THE VERSAILLES SETTLEMENT

Was It Foredoomed to Failure?

PROBLEMS IN EUROPEAN CIVILIZATION

UNDER THE EDITORIAL DIRECTION OF

Ralph W. Greenlaw⁽ᵐ⁾ *and Dwight E. Lee*†

Other volumes in preparation

PROBLEMS IN EUROPEAN CIVILIZATION

THE
VERSAILLES
SETTLEMENT

Was It Foredoomed to Failure?

EDITED WITH AN INTRODUCTION BY

Ivo J. Lederer, YALE UNIVERSITY

D. C. HEATH AND COMPANY · BOSTON

Table of Contents

Introduction

No peace settlement in modern times has stirred greater controversy than the Treaty of Versailles and its related treaties,[1] concluded at the end of World War I by the victorious Allies with the Central Powers: Germany, Austria, Hungary, Bulgaria and Turkey. Indeed, the Versailles settlement has come to mean all things to all men: on the one hand, the triumph of democracy, national self-determination, justice, the rule of law and security against militarism; and on the other hand, the triumph of cynicism, calculated vengeance, economic unrealism and oppression of national minorities.

In reality, the Versailles settlement combined elements of idealism and morality, unique in the history of peacemaking, with old-fashioned power politics. It changed the political map of Europe. In so doing, "Versailles" inevitably had its beneficiaries as well as its victims. The former saw it as the fulfillment of national self-determination; the latter as a grievous *Diktat*. Much has been said for either case. Yet the statesmen of 1919 acted in the belief that they were the first to be governed by principles that would result in fairness for all and an enduring, stable peace.

Peace treaties have by long tradition reflected the imposition of terms, in varying degrees of severity, by victors over vanquished. Force has tended to prevail as the final arbiter of settlements. But losers continued to look to future changes in the ever shifting balance of power for consolation. Wartime defeat and cessions of territory were seldom accepted as final. This pattern can still be observed in the treaty ending the Franco-Prussian War in 1871. The

French protested bitterly, but bowed in the face of defeat while nursing in their hearts the spirit of *revanche*.

When it came time to settle the conflict of 1914–1918, conditions and attitudes had, however, changed. The four-year struggle had been so destructive and widespread that the mere prospect of a future war evoked an overwhelming sense of dread. To forestall such a possibility, Woodrow Wilson, and with him other statesmen, resolved to negotiate a just peace, fair to all sides, in the hope of eliminating the very incentives for war. The elemental passion for revenge and the formula that might makes right were to be set aside in the interests of lasting peace through the application of the principles of national self-determination and democracy. The enormous popular response to Wilson and his proclaimed policies gave dramatic evidence of a new public spirit everywhere.

This approach to peace, however, did not remain unchallenged. A number of responsible statesmen and leaders of the victorious powers doubted the wisdom of such a course. They looked for lasting peace only in a treaty which would create a decisive balance of power in favor of the Allies. Because they saw a weak Germany as the best guarantee for international peace and Allied security, they advocated a policy of weakening the Central Powers through annexations and reparations. In 1871 as in 1815, reparations had been exacted as part of the price of defeat; now in 1919, the advocates of a "powerful" peace justified them as compensation for damages inflicted by a guilty aggressor.

In the peace negotiations which opened in January 1919, these two policies inevitably clashed from the very beginning. The controversy soon became public and was freely joined by conference participants, politicians, journalists, laymen and, not long after, by scholars.

To the historian thus falls the difficult but

[1] The Treaty of Versailles with Germany was signed on June 28, 1919; the treaty of St. Germain with Austria on September 10, 1919; the Treaty of Neuilly with Bulgaria on November 27, 1919; the Treaty of Trianon with Hungary on June 4, 1920; the Treaty of Sèvres with Turkey on August 20, 1920, though it was superseded by the later treaty of Lausanne of July 24, 1923.

vital and challenging task of assessing the nature of the Versailles settlement. Was it just, politically sound, economically capable of fulfillment? Was it indeed the harbinger of a new era of international morality and European stability which many of its advocates so ardently sought? Or were its provisions unduly harsh? Did it in fact sow the seeds of destruction which germinated crisis after crisis and eventually pushed Europe into the abyss of a new war? Was its breakdown caused by the passivity of the victors or by the dynamic resistance of the vanquished? Ultimately, was it foredoomed to failure?

In their quest to find answers to these questions historians have generally taken two lines of approach. On the one hand, they have sought to evaluate the Versailles settlement through the perspective of interwar developments or, more precisely, through a study of the extent to which various treaty provisions were fulfilled or evaded from 1919 to 1939. On the other hand, they have looked for clues through a study of the peace conference itself and the cross-currents of ideas and politics that inter-acted at Paris in 1919.

In the final analysis, the historian's conclusions have been to a large degree shaped by the relative importance he attached to various aspects of the overall settlement. Thus, for example, even though the settlement affected territories in Europe, Africa, Asia, and the Pacific, the problems of German reparations and economic stability have been regarded by many as the central issue arising from the peace conference. Others, by contrast, have shown greater concern with the issue of French military security, the figure of Woodrow Wilson, the concept of national self-determination, or the League of Nations.

Several historians of peace conference and interwar diplomacy have stressed the divergence of the national interests of Great Britain, France, Italy, and the United States as a principal cause of weakness in the final settlement. Yet other schools of thought have looked to the extensive political and territorial changes in Eastern Europe as the most consequential result of the peace settlement. They have viewed the dismantling of the great eastern empires of Austria, Germany, and Russia with favor or apprehension, echoing, as it were, Sir Halford Mackinder's portentous dictum: "Who rules East Europe commands the Heartland; Who rules the Heartland commands the World-Island; Who rules the World-Island commands the World."[2]

Finally, historians have also been seriously concerned with the extent to which the absence of Russia from the peace conference, due to the recent revolution and civil war, created a fateful vacuum in the political structure of Europe. America's withdrawal from European affairs after 1919 and its effect on the European balance of power has given grounds for no lesser concern.

The readings that follow approach the problem of the Versailles settlement through a wide range of points of view, though in the relatively short space available not all could be represented. Interpretive problems connected with Woodrow Wilson, the League of Nations, and the famous question of "war guilt" in Article 231 of the Treaty of Versailles have been omitted entirely.[3] For these and other specific problems, such as those affecting the position of Italy, the reader should consult the _Suggestions for Additional Reading_ at the end of the book.

The opening selection comes from the scholarly pen of Hajo Holborn who places the issues of Versailles into historical perspective. His analysis of these issues serves at the same time as a factual survey of the events of 1918–1920 as well as a synthesis

[2] Sir Halford Mackinder, _Democratic Ideals and Reality_ (London, Constable, 1919), p. 194.

[3] On these problems, readers are referred to the following two titles: Theodore P. Greene, ed., _Wilson at Versailles_ (Boston, 1957), in D. C. Heath's _Problems in American Civilization_ (Amherst) series; and Dwight E. Lee, ed., _The Outbreak of the First World War: Who Was Responsible?_ (Boston, 1958), in D. C. Heath's _Problems in European Civilization_ series.

of the strengths and weaknesses of the over-all settlement.

In Harold Nicolson, whose selection follows directly, the reader will find, in addition to a singularly vivid description of the Paris Peace conference, a notable instance of a British liberal who became bitterly disillusioned with its results. A fervent supporter of Wilsonian concepts of justice and morality, Nicolson became increasingly more critical of the peacemakers of 1919 as they abandoned, in his view, their originally lofty ideals in favor of political compromise.

Nicolson's was indeed the dilemma of many liberals after 1919, though not all shared his sense of pervading disappointment. In fact, despite two decades of growing apprehension about the instability of Europe and an increasing public tendency to attribute it directly to Versailles, the settlement of 1919–1920 was not without its vigorous defenders.

In one of the most noteworthy studies on Versailles, published in the course of World War II, Paul Birdsall undertook the task of re-examining the entire problem in the light of the intervening years. He emerged with a remarkably favorable judgment of the Versailles settlement. Though not uncritical of some of its provisions, Birdsall held steadfastly to the view that the territorial readjustments in Europe in particular were not only politically sound, but also fully consonant with Wilsonian principles of justice.

As applied to Germany the debate has been as lively, since from the moment of the armistice in November 1918 to the outbreak of World War II Germany and the German treaty have been viewed as crucial pillars in the whole edifice of peace. To the French, the *raison d'être* of the war was to halt German expansionism and militarism and to eliminate once and for all any German threat against France. Consequently, they looked to the treaty of peace to create the necessary conditions for the long-range security of France. Their position, as elaborated in the next selection by André

Tardieu, centered on the imposition of stringent military, economic, and territorial terms. In their view, harsh treaty terms were morally and juridically justified by Article 231 of the Treaty of Versailles by which Germany was formally caused to accept full responsibility for "all the loss and damage to which the Allied and Associated Governments and their nationals have been subjected as a consequence of the war imposed upon them by the aggression of Germany and her allies."

Of the over 400 articles of the German treaty, those dealing with the question of reparations have caused the greatest controversy. "Reparations" have been held as responsible for the collapse of the German economy; for the rise of Hitler and Nazism; for weakening inter-allied unity in the years after 1919 and, in part, for alienating the United States from its European allies.

While the controversy concerning German reparations began in the inner committees of the Paris peace conference, it exploded into public view with the publication in 1919 of John Maynard Keynes' famous book, *The Economic Consequences of the Peace.* A brilliant British economist, Keynes charged that the economic features of the German Treaty were so severe as to be incapable of fulfillment.

Almost a quarter century later, a remarkable young French economist, Etienne Mantoux, disputed Keynes' premises with such forceful arguments that they have since come to serve as the most eloquent defense of the economic terms of the treaty of 1919.

Since the United States was a central participant in the negotiations that led to the final reparations terms, the next selection by John Foster Dulles, then attached to the American peace delegation as a senior adviser on economic matters, is of vital importance for an understanding of the way reparations came to be set. Moreover, Dulles also poses important interpretive questions with respect to the American role in the making of the famous Article 231.

The six selections that follow deal at length with the origins, the nature, and the consequences of the territorial settlement in Europe. While it was axiomatic of the Versailles settlement that the vanquished states of Europe would suffer considerable territorial losses, these losses were regarded by the peacemakers as justifiable on grounds of national self-determination, strategic military security, and, in cases of specific localities, economic viability.

It did not seem unreasonable to expect that the losers of World War I would resent territorial losses and, if given the chance, pursue revisionist policies. Such expectations, therefore, gave rise to various diplomatic combinations, led in the main by France, which sought to maintain the status quo of 1919 and the existing balance of power. Yet even the victors were not unanimously satisfied with the territorial settlement. This was due in part to diverging national interests and differing conceptions of allied war aims. Italy, for instance, looked to Austria-Hungary as her principal military adversary. Great Britain and France both looked to Germany as their main common enemy. But while the British were most immediately concerned with the naval and commercial aspects of the German threat, the French, still conscious of their defeat in 1870, were more apprehensive of Germany's military might on land — specifically her military position on the borders of France and in the east.

It is not surprising, therefore, that the territorial settlement reflected some of these inter-allied differences. With respect to Germany's eastern frontiers, Franco-British differences were particularly lively. They are most succinctly brought out in the next selection, by the British scholar W. M. Jordan.

At the same time, the question of Germany's eastern frontiers received significant attention, albeit in entirely different fashion, in Hitler's *Mein Kampf*. Hitler's treatment of this issue is doubly important, for he was not only a leading champion of the revisionist anti-Versailles movement, but also oddly enough, a determined opponent of the German frontiers of 1914 which he regarded as historically fortuitous, militarily useless, and totally inadequate for the future development of Germandom. He explicitly barred a return to the frontiers of 1914 as a basis for the revision of the Treaty of Versailles.

In terms of more general appraisals of the territorial settlements of 1919–1920, one of its staunch defenders in the years between the two wars was Winston Churchill. By contrast to the massive revisionist campaigns then current in Germany, Hungary, Bulgaria, and elsewhere, and here represented in the selections by Hitler, Genov, and Deak, Churchill regarded the territorial changes wrought upon the map of Europe as the central feature of the peace settlement. He also saw them as the consummation of the principle of national self-determination.

Churchill's views fully echoed those of Thomas Masaryk, the great Czechoslovak scholar-statesman. The passages from Masaryk's political memoirs, *The Making of a State*, may be taken as representing a defense of the settlement from the point of view of the newly emerged independent states of Eastern Europe. As such, they are all the more significant because they embody a strong appeal for a new sense of morality in international relations and look upon the settlement as the only basis for future European stability and progress.

The concluding selection by Charles Seymour, member of the American peace delegation in 1919 and distinguished student of American diplomacy, was published in 1951, at a time when general concern with the "cold war" completely overshadowed the issues of Versailles. In it, not unconscious of the very timeliness of the problem, Seymour took a new hard look at the interplay of geography, justice, and politics at Paris in 1919. His conclusions were generally sympathetic to the peace efforts after World War I and in this relatively recent re-evaluation Seymour has rendered a sober and penetrating judgment on the reasons why the peace of Versailles eventually collapsed.

The Conflict of Opinion

"The year 1919 was the high watermark of democracy in world history. . . . Still . . . 'the war to end war' turned out to be the harbinger of even greater disaster. World War I had shown that the balance of power did not exist any longer. . . . The failure to integrate Russia in some fashion into a European system created serious uncertainties. . . . That the Paris settlement did not become a world settlement was also owing to the withdrawal of the United States from Woodrow Wilson's great design."

— HAJO HOLBORN

"The historian, with every justification, will come to the conclusion that we were very stupid men. . . . We arrived determined that a Peace of justice and wisdom should be negotiated: we left it conscious that the Treaties imposed upon our enemies were neither just nor wise . . . the sanctimonious pharisaism of the Treaties is their gravest fault."

— HAROLD NICOLSON

"The territorial settlement in Europe was by no means the wholesale, iniquitous, and cynical perversion of Wilson's principles of self-determination which has been pictured."

— PAUL BIRDSALL

". . . this treaty ignores the economic solidarity of Europe, and by aiming at the economic life of Germany it threatens the health and prosperity of the Allies themselves . . . by making demands the execution of which is in the literal sense impossible, it stultifies itself and leaves Europe more unsettled than it found it."

— JOHN MAYNARD KEYNES

"Mr. Keynes . . . predicted that in the next thirty years, Germany could not possibly be expected to pay more than 2 milliard marks a year in reparation. In the six years preceding September 1939, Germany, by Hitler's showing, had spent each year on rearmament alone about seven times as much. . . . Now . . . while the economic defects of that settlement were, for the most part, illusory or exaggerated, the present writer shares the opinion of those who have maintained that the political defects were the really decisive ones . . . to put it shortly, in the failure, and one might also say, in the deliberate failure, to establish a true *balance of power*."

— ETIENNE MANTOUX

". . . it is by the territorial settlements in Europe that the Treaties of 1919 and 1920 will finally be judged . . . a fair judgment upon settlement, a simple explanation of how it arose, cannot leave the authors of the new map of Europe under serious reproach. To an overwhelming extent the wishes of the various populations prevailed."

— WINSTON CHURCHILL

". . . the Peace Treaties have created juster conditions throughout Europe, and we are entitled to expect that the tension between States and races will decrease."

— THOMAS MASARYK

"The Peace Conference, representing the democracies, reflected the mind of the age; it could not rise measurably above its source. That mind was dominated by a reactionary nostalgia and a traditional nationalism. . . . It was not so much the absence of justice from the Paris Peace Conference that caused the ultimate debacle; it was the failure to make the most of what justice there was."

— CHARLES SEYMOUR

WORLD WAR, WORLD SETTLEMENT AND THE AFTERMATH

HAJO HOLBORN

Hajo Holborn, distinguished scholar in the fields of modern European, German, and diplomatic history, has long been concerned with the study of World War I and its aftermath. A student of the great German historian, Friedrich Meinecke, he left Germany in 1934 for the United States, following a decade of intensive academic activity, and as a result of liberal political convictions which made him an implacable foe of Nazism. His study, *The Political Collapse of Europe,* from which the following passages are drawn, stands out as a singular historical synthesis of the forces which have shaped European politics in the 19th and 20th centuries.

THE BREAKDOWN of the European balance of power during the war years of 1914–17 could not fail to affect the whole world. For Europe was the undisputed political, industrial, and financial center of the earth, and the European nations were locked in an internecine struggle, employing recklessly their rich resources for mutual destruction. What the absence of the European states from other global scenes meant could be learned at once by the new Japanese drive for expansion in the Pacific. The European war also shifted the foundations of American security.

The American Republic had gained its original independence as a result of the division between the two major colonial powers of eighteenth century Europe — Britain and France. The freedom of action enjoyed by the United States in the affairs of the Western hemisphere all through the nineteenth century had rested to a large extent on the rivalries among the European nations which had kept them from large-scale political intervention in the New World. But even more important was the fact that Britain controlled the oceans after 1815 and therefore was able to block the continental European states in any attempted interference with the political fortunes of the New World. American foreign relations through the century prior to 1914 had been chiefly relations with Britain, and events had shown that they could be maintained on a friendly and peaceful level.

But the European war of 1914 threatened to destroy the political system that had made possible America's relative aloofness from world politics during the nineteenth century. If the European Allies had been defeated, the United States would have had to face on the eastern shores of the Atlantic a continent practically united under German leadership. The German alliance with the Turkish empire would have extended Germany's sway to the eastern Mediterranean and the Persian Gulf, and the defeat of Russia would have enabled Germany to draw on the resources of Eurasia. This huge accumulation of power would have been in the hands of a state that in the wartime quarrels over the international law of the seas gave the United States a foretaste of its dictatorial manners. The United States had good reason for associating herself with the Allies at a time when, owing to the impending collapse of Russia, their cause was in acute jeopardy. The American people were hardly aware of these cogent reasons for the entrance of the United States into the war and viewed American participation in it entirely in the light of a crusade for freedom and democracy.

It is even doubtful whether Wilson and his advisers were quite conscious of the pressure of fateful historical circumstances that forced the United States to support the Allies. It was true that the American policy of neutrality toward the European war was from the beginning strongly slanted in favor of Britain, but this policy was never set forth in terms of the American national interest; it was defended by legal theories concerning the maritime rights of neutrals. If the Germans had paid more heed to these American declarations, war between the United States and Germany might have been avoided. . . .

Wilson's Fourteen Points speech and his subsequent speeches on foreign affairs in 1918 became great signposts of a liberal world order. In contrast to the dissipated "psychological" warfare of the Allies in World War II, Allied political warfare in 1918 proved extremely effective, for it was based on a political program that both attracted whole nationalities to the Allied side — some of the component popular groups of the Habsburg empire, for instance — and also held to the defeated foe hope for an ordered international and decent national life. When in the summer of 1918 Germany and Austria-Hungary had to recognize that they could not hope to win the war, when the western front showed signs of breaking and the southeastern front in Turkey and Bulgaria collapsed, even Ludendorff, who had always felt nothing but scorn for the Fourteen Points, saw in them the sheet anchor of a Germany in defeat. The German wartime dictator insisted that Germany should have a parliamentary government and should request an armistice and peace on the basis of the Fourteen Points.

It was the German request for such an armistice, sent to Washington on October 5, that enabled Wilson to bring the question of Allied peace aims to a showdown. The Fourteen Points were not a program to which the European Allies, Britain, France, and Italy, were officially committed. While Wilson tried to exact from Germany further promises of internal democratization and thereby helped to precipitate the outbreak of the German revolution, the struggle for a uniform peace program went on among the Allies in Paris. Britain, France, and Italy were unwilling to commit themselves to the Fourteen Points, and only Colonel House's open warning at the supreme war council in Paris that under such circumstances the United States would proceed to conclude a separate armistice with Germany led to Allied agreement. Point Two, covering the American demand for freedom of the seas, was practically excluded, but the question of reparations, which the Fourteen Points had only sketchily dealt with, was formulated in clear terms, though the British, French, and others boldly challenged the meaning of the text at the peace conference.

By an American note of November 5, 1918, signed by Secretary Lansing, Germany was duly informed of the Allied understanding and, if she accepted the political conditions, invited to dispatch a delegate to Compiègne to receive the military armistice conditions. This military armistice was exclusively French and British in origin. General Pershing advised against granting the Germans an armistice; he wanted the Allied armies to march to Berlin. Foch, considering the grievous losses that the Allies had suffered in four years of cruel fighting, was willing to accept an armistice, provided it secured the military and political objectives of the war. In his opinion, which was shared by other Allied generals, the Allied armies could not reach the Rhine before March, 1919. But if the Germans withdrew behind the Rhine and agreed to hand over a substantial amount of their arms, the Allies would achieve their military objectives without another dreadful winter of fighting and could also impose their political terms, since Germany would be unable to resume the battle. Foch himself considered the control of the Rhineland the supreme war aim of France and tried to secure it through the military armistice that he proposed to the heads of the Allied governments and dictated to the Germans. The British added to the armistice the naval chapters, which practically realized their foremost war aim, namely the destruction of the German navy. When the Germans signed the armistice on November 11th, they surrendered their capacity for resistance by military means to the future political demands of the victors. Nevertheless, the armistice was no unconditional surrender. The victor nations, bound among themselves to the Wilsonian peace program by their Paris agreement, were under an obligation to the defeated nations to construct a liberal peace.

Just prior to the breakdown of Germany's military might the Habsburg empire collapsed. But, whereas Germany, in spite of the occupation and amputation of some of her provinces, continued to be a big state, the Habsburg empire dissolved into a number of states. The demise of the historic empire was the result of the revolt of its various nationalities, of which some, the Yugoslavs, Rumanians, and Poles, wanted to be united with groups or states outside the boundaries of the former empire. Only Czechoslovakia and, of course, Austria and Hungary themselves were "succession states" in the strict sense.

The revival of the nationalities of eastern Europe had begun in the early nineteenth century largely under the influence of the German romanticism that had started with Herder. But when the movement was transformed from one of cultural regeneration into one of political liberation the ideas of the French Revolution and with them the desire for direct political co-operation with the West became more dominant. There were, however, also those who expected their national liberation from Russia. The Serbs, linked to Russia by the same religious faith and similar monarchical institutions, were most hopeful of Russian help: The Croats, Slovenes, and Czechoslovaks welcomed the Russian alliance with the western European powers as a guarantee of victory over the Germans and Magyars, but they wanted to live between the East and West; certainly they did not want to rely exclusively or even predominantly on Russia. The Poles, on the other hand, had hardly any good feelings towards Russia. On the contrary, there were even Poles who felt, after the German victories over Russia, that the creation of a Polish state could be solved in collaboration with Germany; but the German treatment of Poland during World War I and the absolute unwillingness of Germany to consider the status of the Polish provinces of Prussia frustrated any constructive attempt at German-Polish co-operation during World War I. On the whole it could be said that Panslavism was chiefly a sentiment expressing common Slav hostility against Germany; it was not a positive element of unity among the Slavs, and least of all was it an incentive to accepting Russian hegemony.

The defeat of Russia by Germany and the rise of bolshevism orientated all the eastern European nations toward the West, but without turning them into easy followers of the western European powers. Each of them doggedly pursued the goal of its own national independence, disregarding their mutual relations and also the long-range problems of European community life. As soon as the three big powers that had ruled central and eastern Europe for the last centuries collapsed, Czechoslovakia and Poland began to feud; so did Rumania and Poland, and all of them displayed vengeful enmity toward Austria and Hungary, which incidentally, were themselves at odds once the Habsburg monarchy fell.

Britain and France had favored the dissolution of the Habsburg empire early in the war. The Treaty of London of May, 1915, with its lavish promises of Italian gains at the expense of Austria-Hungary, showed that the Allies felt little concern about the future of the Habsburg empire, and in January, 1917, replying to President Wilson's inquiry into the war aims of the belligerents, the Allies publicly stated their support of the Slav and Rumanian national movements. Sympathy with the struggle of the nationalities in the Habsburg empire had originally been aroused at the time of the conclusion of the Anglo-French and the Anglo-Russian ententes by a small group of French and English scholars like Louis Eisenmann, R. W. Seton-Watson, and Wickham Steed. During World War I these men exercised great influence on both sides of the Atlantic through a periodical with the significant title *The New Europe*.

The entrance of the United States into the war put temporary brakes upon the drive for full independence of the southeastern nationalities. American diplomacy hoped to reach a separate peace with Austria-Hungary. Even the Fourteen Points speech of January 8, 1918, proclaimed America's desire to see Austria-Hungary's place among the nations "safeguarded and assured," though her people "should be accorded the freest opportunity of autonomous development." But the failure of the secret peace negotiations with the Government of Emperor Charles of Austria-Hungary induced the United States to throw her full weight behind the disruptive national forces. The curious *de jure* recognition of the Czechoslovak committee of Masaryk and Beneš, which was not even a *de facto* government of Bohemia and Moravia, was the final seal of this policy. The military collapse of Germany and Austria-Hungary led to the dissolution of the Habsburg empire and the rise of the new states all along the eastern fringe of Europe from Finland to Yugoslavia. When the Paris Peace Conference convened in January, 1919, the political map of Europe had already been radically changed.

The year 1919 was the high watermark of democracy in world history. Not even 1945 can be compared to that year, since in 1945 the democratic nations shared their victory with the Soviet Union and the major spoils of victory went to the latter. In 1919 no autocratic or authoritarian power could obstruct the peace settlement, and peacemaking was the exclusive responsibility of the democratic nations. Still, "the war to make the world safe for democracy," a phrase first coined by H. G. Wells in August, 1914, to describe the meaning of World War I, brought forth before long the age of the dictators, and "the war to end war" turned out to be the harbinger of even greater disaster.

If we compare the Paris settlement of 1919 to the Vienna settlement of 1815, it is obvious that some of the fundamental elements that made for unity and mutual understanding among the peacemakers of Vienna were lacking in 1919. The wars of 1812–15 had a clear common aim, the defeat of Napoleon's revolutionary attempt at uniting the Continent under his dictatorial power and the restoration of the old European state system. The war of 1914–18 did not have such a single common goal. Of course, the immediate objective of the war, the destruction of Germany's overweaning power, was accepted as a general Allied war aim, but no clarity existed among the victorious powers about the type of Europe that they wanted to build or rebuild, supposing, indeed, that they could construct a European political system at all.

World War I had shown that the balance of Europe did not exist any longer; in order to subdue the Central Powers the intervention of the United States and also of the British dominions was required. The United States played a leading, and the British dominions a significant, role in the making of the peace settlement of Paris in 1919. It was natural that they wished to create a world settlement and that they were little concerned about the resurrection of the broken-down European system. The British Government, owing to its own world-wide commitments, easily fell in with this trend. In contrast, Clemenceau, more than any other Allied statesman, thought in terms of the restoration of a European balance of power and made a supreme effort to gain a peace that would place France in an unassailable position of military superiority over Germany. He therefore aimed at the amputation of a maximum of German territories, the blocking of the merger of Austria and Germany, the imposition of heavy reparations, and French control of the left bank of the Rhine.

To the rigid military mind of General Foch this program was the logical expression of French national interest; but Clemenceau himself was too wise to look at politics in such simple logical terms. The last great Jacobin knew the dynamic force of nationalism and realized that a treaty of this description would breed fiery German resentment. It was doubtful, furthermore, whether France by herself could make such a peace settlement effective. France would have succumbed to Germany in the war if it had not been for her Allies, and she had suffered grievous losses that not even victory could recover. Clemenceau was under no illusion that the future security of France did not depend principally on continued co-operation with Britain and the United States.

Although Clemenceau bargained hard to gain the French points, he compromised with Wilson and Lloyd George on the Rhineland issue. France received no German territory outside of Alsace-Lorraine. The Saar district was separated from Germany and France given a preponderant position in its administration, but it was to be under League auspices and a plebiscite was to take place after fifteen years to settle the final status of the region according to the wishes of its inhabitants. No separate Rhenish state was created, and though the Rhineland was demilitarized, its occupation by Allied troops was limited to fifteen years. In exchange for these stipulations made possible by Clemenceau's concessions, France was promised that if during the next fifteen years the Germans were to challenge the arrangements concerning the Rhineland, the United States and Britain would give her military assistance.

The most crucial of all the political problems of Europe was thus settled by arrangements that envisaged the continued participation of a non-European power in the maintenance of the European peace. In the Rhineland this co-operation took the form of a specific guarantee by individual nations. In general the universal League of Nations, composed of members from all continents, was supposed to safeguard the peace of Europe as a part of world peace. No conscious attempt was made to reconstruct a politically self-sufficient European system. Nobody could contend that a Europe similar to that of the nineteenth century could have been revived by the Paris Peace Conference, and the conference dealt almost exclusively with the claims of nations on the one hand and with the building of a world system on the other. The common problems concerned with Europe as a whole found no discussion.

No other political document could have offered as much guidance for the establishment of a peaceful international society as did the American constitution, and it was the greatness of Woodrow Wilson that he projected the American political tradition ably and eloquently into a liberal international faith. The weakness of Wilson's international program lay in the generality of many of its tenets and in the contradictory nature of some of them. The principle of national self-determination, for example, was not universally practicable, and in certain cases it conflicted with other Wilsonian principles, such as the demand of access to the seas for landlocked states. The generality of the Fourteen Points and their lack of absolute logical unity offered the opportunity for perverting Wilson's program at the peace conference by writing many nationalistic war gains into the final settlement. But with more good will Wilson's program could have been adapted to the historic conditions of the hour.

More serious was Wilson's ingrained belief that his abstract ideals could blot out certain realities of political life. Walter Lippmann once pointed out that the Wilsonian principles were formulated on the basis of America's aloofness from world politics as it had existed due to specific and fortunate historical circumstances. "Wilson wished America to take its place in a universal society. But he was willing to participate only if the world acted as the United States had acted when it enjoyed isolation during the 19th century." In reality, America, too, had entered world politics since the Spanish-American War and the building of the Panama Canal. Although Wilson, ever since he had become president in 1912, had earnestly tried to keep the United States out of world conflicts, the great European crisis of 1914 and its consequences had forced him to lead the country into the war. Strategic considerations of more than local and even more than hemispheric scope were no longer alien to American foreign policy.

But how deeply Woodrow Wilson was steeped in the political sentiment of the happy earlier period can be seen for example from his Point Four: "Adequate guarantees given and taken that national armaments will be reduced to the lowest point consistent with domestic safety." The navy "second to none" that the United States was building since 1916 could not be defined as one protecting exclusively "domestic safety," though the American peacetime army could be so described. To the continental states of Europe, land forces were their first and last line of defense. It was utterly unrealistic to ask them to be satisfied with mere frontier guards and police forces. Wilson had soon recognized this himself, and Article 8, the principle article of the League Covenant dealing with disarmament, spoke only of the reduction of national armaments to the lowest point "consistent with national safety and the enforcement by common action of international obligations." "Geographical situation and circumstances of each state" were to be taken into account in the formulation of the disarmament plans of the League. These were sensible provisions, but it was unfortunate that in the meantime the

German disarmament conditions imposed by the Treaty of Versailles were linked up with the future international disarmament that the League of Nations was to inaugurate. As the preamble of part V of the Versailles Treaty of Versailles put it: "In order to render possible the initiation of a general limitation of the armaments of all nations, Germany undertakes strictly to observe the military, naval, and air clauses which follow." The disarmament clauses of Versailles were no doubt a rather literal application of Wilson's Point Four, but not of Article 8 of the Covenant toward which the preamble gratuitously and mistakenly pointed.

The history of disarmament at the Paris Peace Conference can serve as a good illustration of the great distance that had to be travelled in order to translate the Wilsonian ideals into practical political arrangements. On the other hand, it offers an example of how eager Wilson was to justify concrete decisions as emanations from absolute principles. There was in Wilson's philosophy, however, a grave misunderstanding of the relation between abstract ideas and power in history. Wilson was deeply convinced that the proclamation of liberal ideals in international life would everywhere rally the common man to their support. In this sense he could say to the American delegation on his way to Paris that only he, and not Lloyd George and Clemenceau, represented the people. But in the formal sense Clemenceau and Lloyd George represented their nations more fully than Woodrow Wilson. He had lost control of Congress in the November elections, and it was unpredictable what opposition his foreign policy might meet at home in the future. In contrast, Lloyd George had called for British elections in December and had gained a strong, if unwieldy, parliamentary majority, while the French Chamber of Deputies had voted 4:1 in favor of Clemenceau after he presented on December 27, 1918, his plans for French policy at the approaching peace conference. Clemenceau was openly hostile to Wilsonian idealism, and the British "khaki elections" were fought by Lloyd George and his liberal and conservative party friends with nationalistic slogans that contradicted the Government's official acceptance of the Wilsonian program. The Asquith-Grey liberals, who from 1906 to 1916 had dominated British policy and in whose circles many of the Wilsonian ideas had been born, were crushed by the jingoistic temper of the British election campaign.

Still, Wilson's program appealed to the common man, and the popular ovations that he received everywhere he went in Europe were genuine. To almost everybody it seemed that the program offered a way to end the cruel bloodshed and to cure the wounds that four years of war had inflicted on all national societies. It promised gains to all the allied powers, at the same time promising Germany as well as Austria and Hungary the protection of the principle of nationality. The Wilsonian program had a twofold root and double purpose. It was not only a design of an international peace settlement but also an instrument of political warfare. And as a political weapon it proved a complete success during 1918. It gave hope to the Allied nations in the early months of the year when they reeled under the blows of the German spring offensive in the West, it rallied the separatist national movements in the Habsburg empire to the support of the Allied cause, and it strengthened the peace sentiment in the enemy countries. American political warfare made a great contribution to the early winning of World War I.

But the immediate impact of American propaganda on Europe was the strengthening of national sentiment. To gain or regain full national independence and the strongest possible military strength to defend it was the dearest objective of every warring European nation. The internationalism of Wilson was shared by the European statesmen only in so far as it did not deny them the full realization of their own nationalistic aims. In Wilson's eyes national self-determination was a means to lay grievances to

rest and thus a direct step towards a peaceful international society. To most Europeans the satisfaction of their national dreams was an absolute end, even when their realization violated the national self-determination of others.

Shortsighted as this policy was — and more will be said about it later — the desire of the European states, old and new, to gain national security through a maximum of power, which they measured by area and population, was to some degree understandable. As early as January, 1917, Wilson had proclaimed that there should be no "new balance of power," but instead a "community of power." His concept of a League of Nations, however, though it envisaged the ultimate use of force against an aggressor, rested chiefly on the belief that a united world opinion would act as a deterrent to aggression and that, if this failed, an aggressor could probably be brought to heel by economic boycott and blockade. Collective military action was to be taken, if at all, only after considerable damage had been done. Yet defense against invasion was still a vital problem that the individual states alone or in groups would have to meet. Although Wilson was right when he judged that the balance of power had failed to provide a secure foundation for world peace, the different nations, including the United States and Britain, were far from ready to pool their whole strength in a single "community of power," and the relative balance of power between states remained a matter of vital significance. The League of Nations of 1919 was not what its English name said it was, a closely united group of states ready for immediate concerted action. The French name *Société des Nations* described the nature of the organization more aptly.

If the League of Nations was to gain true life, its roots had to sink deeply into the soil of national security interests. Such a policy would have required the frank recognition of the balance of power that Wilson rejected. In his opinion the struggle for power had come to an end with the armistice, and the peacemakers should now settle all claims largely on the basis of universally valid principles. Such an attitude was bound to lead to great embarrassment. Inevitably, Wilson had to make continuous concessions to the balance of power. One of the first, made shortly after his arrival in Europe, was his consent to Italy's obtaining the Brenner Pass frontier, in stark contrast to his own Point Nine, which had demanded "a readjustment of the frontiers of Italy . . . along clearly recognizable lines of nationality."

To be sure, a case could be made for giving Italy a strong strategic frontier to the north in disregard of the quarter million Austrians living south of the Brenner if Austria was to be joined to Germany. Even Hitler in *Mein Kampf* and later on, from 1933–43, at least, accepted the Brenner line. But the Paris conference of 1919 prohibited the *Anschluss,* and it was difficult to see why Wilson would accept Italy's demand for the annexation of South Tyrol yet stubbornly oppose her Adriatic claims. This concession, like that made over disarmament, which has been discussed already, brought Wilson's high principles under a cloud of suspicion. It was not wise to use these ideals as the justification of actions that were plainly decisions on power relationships and that could not be avoided if one wanted an agreement among the powers to make peace. By Wilson's insistence on wrapping up necessary compromises in the language of general principles, his ideals lost much of the radiance that would have made them steady beacons in the evolution of a collective system. Abused ideals have a tremendous aptitude for vengeance. The difficulty during the interwar period of arousing strong popular support for the forceful maintenance of the Paris settlement was largely due to the fact that the intellectual and moral foundation of the peace appeared to be very weak.

This is not to say that all the concessions that the peace conference made to nationalistic demands could be called practical decisions. Actually many of them were patently obnoxious. But the elementary longing of the states for security could not be disregarded or met only surreptitiously. Yet it could have been pointed out to them that no European state had ever enjoyed security in isolation and that in spite of all her wars and divisions Europe had managed in the past to restore a communal life after every crisis through which she had gone. The statesmen of the Congress of Vienna had speedily welcomed France back to the European concert without neglecting to take those precautionary measures that kept France from renewing her career of Napoleonic conquest. In the absence of general wars during the later nineteenth century the existence of neutral great powers had exercised a restraining influence upon the victor in a war. But none of these curative forces seemed to have survived the holocaust of World War I in Europe.

Formerly the monarchs and nobility had formed an upper stratum of European society. No doubt, their cupidity had caused many wars, but the similarity of outlook and interest within the group had made bargaining and compromise possible. Woodrow Wilson expected that democracy would be a better maker and guarantor of peace than monarchs and noble elites. Yet this expectation was not fulfilled in 1919.

For one thing, "democratic" foreign policy was in its infancy. Prior to World War I even people in states with a popular constitution paid little attention to the actual conduct of foreign affairs except in periods of tension. Britain had the oldest tradition of parliamentary control, and the British parties, it is true, usually identified themselves with differing foreign policies. In fact British foreign policy often changed with changing parliamentary majorities. Within these limitations, however, the prime minister and foreign secretary in 1905–06 after the Liberal victory at the polls, decided to accept the foreign policy of his predecessor. Continuity of British foreign policy was gained by this action, but not necessarily greater popular participation. Organizations like the Union of

Democratic Control and personalities like Edmund D. Morel and James Bryce attempted to arouse public interest in a fuller parliamentary and popular control of foreign affairs and particularly in the suppression of secret diplomacy, but the movement did not make much progress in Britain. It won many adherents in the United States, however; much of the Wilsonian concept of democratic foreign policy, including his belief in "open diplomacy," stemmed from the thought of some of these British reformers.

Thus during World War I the groups of people who were able to think about international affairs competently and with a reasonable detachment from national emotions were small in all countries and demagogy could flourish. The Americans exercised a moderating influence in a good many European matters, but they were handicapped by the political death of the old British Liberal party, with which they could have established better working relations than with Lloyd George, who, though a liberal, had made himself highly vulnerable to nationalistic pressures.

Wilson might have been in better position to modify some of the excesses of nationalism if he could have broadened the scope of the conference debates. Everybody agreed that the political world settlement would require for its support a restoration of world trade and world economy. But the American delegation was not in a position to discuss the revival of a free and stable economy in a comprehensive and systematic fashion.

Four groups of economic problems existed in 1919. There were first the urgent relief needs in the provinces of the Central Powers and the countries that they had occupied during World War I. Second, the world faced the difficulty of rehabilitating Europe's productivity and working out a program of economic development for the new eastern European states. Third, there were the problems arising from the economic transformations that had been brought about by the great expansion during the war of non-European industries and the sudden rise of the United States as the big creditor nation in the world, particularly of Europe. Fourth, there was the difficulty of making a financial settlement between victors and vanquished nations or, more correctly, between the victors and Germany, since the Habsburg empire had disappeared.

The first problems, those of relief, were met. There was some delay due to American insistence on the dissolution of the Allied economic wartime councils after the armistice. Herbert Hoover expressed the American point of view most forcefully when he said that everything should be avoided that would give even the appearance that other powers had a voice in the assignment of American resources. Yet, although most funds and foodstuffs came from the United States, the contribution of the British Commonwealth was by no means negligible, and it was in any case politically unwise to break up the common front, at least prior to the conclusion of peace. New inter-Allied organizations were finally set up in January 1919, under the Supreme Economic Council, over which Lord Robert Cecil presided with Herbert Hoover, who was director general of relief.

The work done under Herbert Hoover's direction and continued after the peace by American private organizations was most effectively executed. It laid the ground for a humane link between the New and the Old World, which gave all American dealings with Europe thereafter a warmer tone. Though this relief action was originally planned only as a humanitarian measure, it was soon to be recognized to be also a means of keeping Bolshevism from flooding central Europe. Before long the Allies decided also on a relaxation of the blockade of Germany, continuation of which they had written into the armistice of November 11, 1918, although Britain and the United States had to overcome French hesitation and also original German resistance to the reasonable conditional demands for the use of German shipping and monetary funds.

The difference between relief and rehabilitation is a relative one. No doubt, the Allied relief activities in Europe after 1919 were of crucial significance for the restoration of normal economic production; but European recovery proved a process of many years, since the problems of the second and third groups were never tackled. Wilson was aware that it was necessary to give the political settlement an economic underpinning, but we may question whether he had a clear conception of the way by which this could be done. His Point Three, for instance, demanding the removal of all economic barriers and the establishment of an equality of trade conditions, had been a rather simple expression of his liberal faith. But it had come under strong fire from the United States Senate and was in these debates reinterpreted by the Wilson Administration in such a fashion as to become practically meaningless.

Wilson seemed, indeed, to have resigned himself to a situation that did not allow him to commit the United States to a definite plan for the reconstruction of world economy, much less for special projects of European recovery and development. He did not think it politically possible to discuss even the settlement of the inter-Allied war debts in this light. The British, who had given their Allies as many loans as they had received from the United States, early proposed to study the problem of international payments, including inter-Allied debts and German reparations, as one affecting the whole future of world economy. They indicated, too, that they were willing to cancel some of the loans that they had made to their Allies in order to help the war effort if their own debts received similar consideration from the United States. But the American delegation at Paris insisted that the American war loans, as enacted by Congress, had been made to individual states on a strict business basis. They could be settled only by negotiations between the United States Government and the individual states. The discussion of inter-Allied debts was thus excluded from the peace conference, and with this decision the opportunity was missed for rebuilding the international economy on a stable foundation.

German reparations consequently was the only major economic problem taken up by the peace conference. In retrospect it is easy to say that nobody, including such critics of the Versailles settlement as John Maynard Keynes or, for that matter, such able financial experts of the German delegation as Carl Melchior, were right in their estimate of the reparations that Germany was able to pay. Everybody overrated Germany's capacity, which was not surprising, since there was no precedent for international payments of comparable magnitude. But if one thing could have been foreseen, it was the close interrelation between any international payments, whether German reparations or inter-Allied debts, and the future development of world economy. If international trade had expanded far beyond the volume of 1913 and if in particular creditor nations had been willing to receive greatly increased imports from debtor countries, much larger sums might have been transferred.

The attempt to set down Germany's capacity for making financial reparations was bound to fail. Only a flexible scheme could have succeeded. But as it was, the Allies wanted a definitive plan of German reparations that would take care not only of the actual war damage but also of the debts that they had incurred in fighting Germany. Britain was particularly anxious; for under a strict interpretation of the definition of German reparations contained in the Lansing note of November 5, 1918, Britain could have claimed reparations only for shipping losses, which were actually paid by the delivery of German vessels, and for the relatively small damage suffered by some English cities as a consequence of naval or air attack.

Leaving aside shipping losses, Britain could have collected only 1 or 2 per cent of German money payments. But the British representatives argued, and General Smuts finally convinced Woodrow Wilson, that war pensions could be considered civilian damages that Germany was liable to repair. The financial bill presented to Germany was thereby tripled. However, since Germany in the end paid even less than a third of the contemplated sum, the size of the reparations was not so important as their new distribution among the Allies; Britain now claimed 22 per cent.

The Paris Peace Conference failed to make systematic plans for world recovery that would have solidified their political arrangements. The Paris peace treaties were a diplomatic peace settlement similar to the Vienna settlement, though, of course, the political philosophies of the two differed. Wilson sensed that security of nationality and frontiers was not enough and that economic and social problems as well demanded the attention of the modern statesmen. The creation of the International Labor Office was an indication of such awareness. Yet the depth of the revolutionary changes that World War I had caused in the social structure and the attitude of nations was hidden from the view of the peacemakers.

Broadly speaking, the wars of earlier times had been wars of armies — armies of restricted, if expanding, numbers limited in their arms and equipment. But World War I had a different character. Formerly the production of Arms ceased when the war broke out, but after 1916 industrial mobilization became as gigantic as the military levies. The civilians were contributing as much to the war as the soldiers, and the endless casualty lists, invasions, and blockade brought the war home to every person in Europe and Russia. In other words, after 1916 World War I turned into the first modern total war. The impact of this event was greatest in Russia, which tried a total mobilization but broke down under the burden. Germany achieved a rather complete government-directed war economy, the first planned economy in modern history.

Nobody in Paris fully realized the por-

tents of the new age. The peace conferences of Vienna and Paris can be compared in many respects. But they took place at very different moments in history. Vienna was the settlement of twenty-odd years of general war, in which the revolutionary forces had been able to modify, but not to overthrow, the old order of Europe. In contrast, the Paris conference was a first attempt at dealing with a new situation that had begun to unfold during the war itself. It was admitted that the world had become *one* world, and a League of Nations was created. But it was a weak league, and in spite of its unassuming character it had yet to gain universality of membership. The Paris Peace Conference also carried diplomatic activities into the economic and social fields, but it did so in an irregular fashion. That the conditions resulting from total war demand for their cure total diplomacy was not yet recognized. Not even today, thirty years later, is it undisputed popular knowledge.

The Paris peace treaties were considered to constitute a world settlement; but they never did. The peace conference could do little about the problems of the Far Eastern Pacific except distribute the German colonies located in that area. But of even greater consequence was its failure to deal with Bolshevist Russia. This is not to suggest that a solution of the Russian problem would have been simple or even possible in 1919. The French were stubbornly opposed to any diplomatic contacts with the Bolshevists, whom they judged to be tools of the Germans and traitors of Russian political and financial commitments to the West. Opposed, also, was Winston Churchill, then the British secretary for war. But the West was unable to intervene in the Russian civil war except by giving arms and other implements of war to the White Russian groups fighting in various parts of Russia against the Bolshevists entrenched in Moscow and St. Petersburg. Few Allied soldiers were willing to be sent to Russia, since after the German armistice everybody was convinced that the fighting was over and that Allied war aims had been achieved.

Winston Churchill, in his Boston speech of March 31, 1949, characterized the "failure to strangle Bolshevism at its birth and to bring Russia . . . by one means or another into the general democratic system" as one of the great mistakes of Allied statesmen in 1919. This statement seems historically correct, and Churchill deserves credit for having seen in 1919 the loss and danger to Europe involved in the isolation of a hostile Russia. . . .

The failure to integrate Russia in some fashion into a European system created serious uncertainties about the future of the Continent. To be sure, for about a decade or more after the revolution, Russia was too weak to exercise any strong direct influence on Europe beyond the ideological impact of the Third International. But the existence of an independent Communist Russian state that controlled an international political movement made the whole European settlement unsafe. The Communist movement intensified everywhere the social unrest that followed in the wake of the peace settlement of Paris, and the Russian state encouraged every nation willing to resist the peace treaties of 1919.

During the nineteenth century Russia had held important non-Russian territories and had wielded great influence in general European affairs. Yet at the same time Europe had not lacked power over Russia. As has been seen, Russian expansion had been kept within certain bounds, and she had been compelled to respect international treaties. Her internal development had been heavily dependent upon foreign capital and technological advice. European ideas had deeply stirred Russian intellectual life. Even the slavophile movement in Russia cannot be understood without consideration of the impact of Western thought. Russia had been "westernized" in many respects and in this process had displayed an unusual capacity for blending her own cultural heritage with modern Western ideas. In the last third of the nineteenth century the great Russian novel and Russian music had become in their turn a leaven in western European thinking.

This political and cultural *rapprochement* between Europe and Russia came to an end with the Russian Revolution. It should be remembered, however, that Marxism is not a native Russian doctrine, though in the hands of Lenin, and even more so of Stalin, it was adapted to the circumstances and needs of a Russia plunged into chaos and misery by military defeat. The philosophy of Karl Marx is an arsenal from which many political schools can draw arms. Bolshevist theory itself has undergone considerable changes since 1917 in response to new political developments. In the early years after the Revolution the Western powers might well have moulded the circumstances that conditioned the evolution of that theory. But this opportunity, if it ever existed, was missed. The new Soviet state grew up in isolation, yet it could not fail to exercise a disruptive influence upon the European order created in Paris, the more so since Moscow ruled not only the Russian empire, now being quickly industrialized and unified in all its parts, but also the International Communist movement.

That the Paris settlement did not become a world settlement was also owing to the withdrawal of the United States from Woodrow Wilson's great design. This withdrawal was not caused by popular dissatisfaction with the treatment meted out by the Paris peace treaties to the vanquished enemies. In so far as the Senate's opposition was more than a display of partisan spirit, it centered around the fear of seeing the United States sucked into an international system whose obligations — if they were clearly understood at all — were dreaded by many Americans. In retrospect it may be asked whether Wilson's adamant insistence on the American ratification of the full Covenant showed good political judgment. Probably even an amended and watered-down Covenant acceptable to the United States Senate would have been preferable to a Covenant rejected by it, since the

United States could then have been in contact with the unfolding European situation.

But even the rejection of the Covenant by the United States might not have been a major catastrophe if America had backed the Mutual Assistance Pact for the Rhine settlement. Theodore Roosevelt and Senators Lodge and Knox felt that it would be better to build any future American participation in world affairs around the practical experience already gained. In their opinion the wartime alliance with the Allied nations ought to be the nucleus of any future American co-operation in international affairs. Thus they were ready to subscribe to the Rhine pact rather than to the League of Nations Covenant. From both an American and a universal point of view, it would have been desirable to have the United States join in the establishment of a world organization for the maintenance of peace; but an American guarantee of the crucial western European frontiers could have been equally decisive. In the fierce party struggle between the President and the Senate both possibilities were lost, and the subsequent neglect of international affairs makes one wonder whether or not the American people would in any case have given their support to international commitments for any length of time.

The United States withdrew from world affairs in 1920 as suddenly as it had appeared on the world scene three years before. This retreat was not complete, since the United States continued to care about a settlement of the Far Eastern issues and was soon drawn again into some sort of co-operation with the European powers in financial matters. Prior to 1914, the United States had been a debtor nation — that is foreign investments in America outbalanced American investments abroad. The liquidation of European holdings in America, however, and the big American loans to the European Allies during World War I and in the armistice period made the United States the chief creditor nation, which it has remained ever since. In the period

between 1920 and 1933 the country was concerned about its European loans and investments, which greatly increased after 1925, when a seemingly stabilized Europe appeared to offer splendid opportunities for American surplus capital.

Even so, the United States after 1920 felt that it could return to its nineteenth-century insularity. Its isolationism became economic as well as diplomatic. The postwar depression led to the Fordney-McCumber Tariff of 1922, and the Hawley-Smoot Tariff of 1930 carried protection to greater heights than ever before. Indeed, all postwar tariffs, of which the American tariffs were only the most outstanding examples, tended to aim at a restoration of the prewar pattern of world economy. But this economy had been irrevocably changed by the World War; Europe could pay her debts to America only if she were allowed to send her products and goods to the United States.

Europe after 1920 was left alone to cope with her political problems. It appeared at once doubtful that she would be able to do so. Quite apart from the great financial and economic questions, which could have been solved only by world-wide arrangements, the whole European scene as envisaged by the peacemakers while they still acted in concert was drastically changed by America's withdrawal. France was immediately affected. She had foregone her demands for a separation of the Rhineland in exchange for an Anglo-American guarantee of the demilitarization of the left bank of the Rhine. The great French concessions at the Peace conference now seemed to have been made in vain.

France was particularly alarmed by the British refusal to sign the mutual guarantee pact. It was true that the Anglo-French treaty as drafted in Paris depended on the willingness of the United States to subscribe to a parallel treaty. The British decision to drop the treaty was no breach of promise, but it was a grave error of judgment. The Rhine was the natural defense line of Britain as much as of France, as World War I had abundantly shown. If

Britain declined to co-operate without reservation in the defense of the Rhine, the French had reasons to distrust the good intentions or the good judgment of British policy. Were the British, once they had achieved the full realization of their war aims — the destruction of Germany as a naval and colonial power — determined to leave the Continent unprotected? France therefore proceeded to build up a system of alliances with the eastern European states.

It was dubious from the beginning whether the new eastern states would be able to live between the Soviet Union and Germany if neither were integrated in some fashion into a European system. Actually, many people forgot Russia altogether. To them Poland seemed to have taken the place that Russia had occupied in Europe before 1914, while Czechoslovakia, Yugoslavia, and Rumania, which formed in 1920–21 alliances chiefly directed against a restoration of Habsburg rule in Hungary, were considered to constitute a substitute for the Habsburg empire. But neither this group of states, called the Little Entente, nor Poland could compare to the former Habsburg or Romanov empires.

It must suffice here to mention only a few of the major weaknesses of the new eastern states. Since they looked in many different directions, toward the Baltic, the Adriatic, Aegean, and Black Seas, they had not much unity among themselves. Furthermore, the Habsburg empire, in spite of its pernicious internal controversies, had formed a viable economic entity, but the new states were confronted with unsolvable economic problems in addition to their formidable political difficulties. Of them all, Czechoslovakia was the most democratic and prosperous. Practically none of the others ever acquired an economic or political equilibrium. They were driven to adopt governmental methods that had only a superficial resemblance to democracy, and their living standards remained far below the European average. The ensuing social crisis, brought to a head by the depression of the late twenties, again inflamed the conflict of nationalities. Not only did states like Poland and Czechoslovakia continue to be at loggerheads, but issues of nationality also undermined the internal cohesion of these two countries as well as Yugoslavia. Hungary, smarting under her defeat, kept revisionist forces alive with the support of fascist Italy.

Consequently, it was an illusion to conceive of the Little Entente and Poland as substitutes for the empires of the Romanovs and Habsburgs. Between 1887 and 1917 France had spent about sixteen billion francs in loans and investments in order to build up her Russian ally. If she could have employed similar amounts of money to set the new eastern states on the road toward prosperity, the system of French eastern alliances might have become a strong underpinning of the European *status quo*. But the French depositor, having lost more than a quarter of all his foreign investments as a result of the World War, was not inclined to permit his government to conduct a bold foreign economic policy. Instead, since the new states remained economically weak, their foremost customer, Germany, continued to hold considerable power in the eastern and southeastern states.

Naturally, the military agreements between France and the eastern states were practical only as long as France was physically capable of co-operating with these allies and making a substantial contribution to their defense both against Germany and the Soviet Union. This co-operation required the disarmament of Germany at least sufficient to permit French troops to force a junction with the Czechoslovak army along a line from Metz-Diedenhofen to Eger-Pilsen. It also called for an army capable of strategic maneuver and not one almost exclusively designed for defensive operations along the frontiers of France.

Actually, France was not in a position to uphold the treaties by her own strength, but in the years immediately following the War she seemed stronger than she really was. The postwar depression, which affected the United States and Britain very severely, hardly touched France, owing to the reconstruction work going on in the war-devastated French provinces. Moreover, although at the end of 1918 the British army and air force were probably stronger than the French services, British armed strength was dissolved with amazing speed. In 1920, needing military strength in India and the Middle East, and in Ireland, the British army of around 300,000 men could spare only 13,000 men for occupation duty in the Rhineland and nothing but a few battalions to help in the policing of the plebiscite areas in upper Silesia and East Prussia, though British diplomacy had been responsible for having these plebiscites instituted. By contrast the French army seemed powerful.

The inequality in mobilized military strength added to the air of unreality that surrounded Franco-British relations in the early years after the war. The two powers even indulged in unfriendly squabbles in the Near East. But the French were chiefly worried by the thought that with the return to a small professional army the British would be incapable of assisting them in gaining security — for them the real prize of the war. France wished to see any future war fought east of the French borders and brought to a quick decision there. If Germany could invade France again or if a war should last long enough to enable Germany to mobilize her superior manpower and industrial potential, France would be destroyed again. A simple promise by Britain, as finally offered by Lord Curzon in 1922, that she would consider any demilitarization of the Rhineland an act of aggression seemed to Frenchmen an inadequate insurance as long as Britain did not provide military forces ready to act instantaneously with the French army in the case of any threat.

Poincaré between 1922 and 1924 attempted to employ the preponderant might of France for the achievement of a European position in which France would no longer have to rely on British support. The occupation of the Ruhr in January, 1923, was undertaken to make Germany pay reparations or, in the case of German opposition, to secure the productive resources that would recompense France. In spite of German "passive resistance" French policy was successful in finally forcing Germany to come to terms; but France as a result of her exertions, was financially exhausted and could not impose her own conditions. American and British intervention instituted the Dawes Plan, which for a period of five years removed reparations from the agenda of European diplomacy. More important, France recognized that she could conduct an independent European policy, but would have to act in close co-operation with Britain, even at the sacrifice of some French advantages and hopes.

It is doubtful that Britain after World War I had a clear conception of the future of Europe. In less than a year after the signing of the Treaty of Versailles she developed, if not a new European policy, at least a new attitude toward European problems. Britain had been severely jolted by her inability, in conjunction with her European allies, to bring the war against the Central Powers to a victorious conclusion. America's intervention had been necessary to decide the war, and the United States proposed to maintain thereafter a navy of a size equal to the British navy. The withdrawal of the United States from European affairs was profoundly alarming to Britain, and the new world situation seemed to make it unwise to assume international obligations as far-reaching as those she had accepted prior to 1914.

The strong support that Britain had received from her dominions during the War had created a warm feeling of unity among the members of the British Commonwealth of Nations; but the British dominions were even more deeply disturbed by America's refusal to join in the guarantee of the Paris settlement than Britain herself. They contributed to the watering down of the Covenant's provisions for automatic sanctions and kept warning Britain against involvement in the problems peculiar to

Europe. The exact influence of dominion opinion on British foreign policy would be difficult to measure, since Britain had reasons of her own for keeping aloof from European engagements. In the 1930's one could not help feeling that the British Government often used the dominions as an easy excuse for its own lack of decision in European affairs. Actually, the policy of the British dominions went through an evolution toward collectivism in international affairs, largely as a reaction to Japanese and Italian expansionism.

Although the Commonwealth became after World War I sentimentally more important to Britain than full participation in a European political system, obvious security needs and economic necessity made it impossible for her to withdraw from the European continent. European recovery was an absolute prerequisite for the restoration of a prosperous British economy, which, in turn, hinged on the revival of German productivity. At the same time, under the leadership of the great economic thinker John Maynard Keynes the British underwent a sudden and violent revulsion from the Paris Peace Treaties. Keynes' treatise *The Economic Consequences of the Peace Treaty,* brilliantly penned, produced an instantaneous and profound public reaction as few political pamphlets in history have ever achieved. Most British people soon agreed that the most serious problems "were not political or territorial but financial and economic, and that the perils of the future lay not in frontiers and sovereignties but in food, coal and transport." Yet this judgment was at best a dangerous half-truth; political security and economic prosperity were equally important and interdependent. Keynes claimed more inside knowledge of the political workings of the Paris Conference than he actually possessed, and his anger at the economic errors that the conference had committed carried him into acrimonious accusations that defeated some of his own aims. He considered, for example, Anglo-American co-operation a precondition of world recovery. But his

venomous portrait of Woodrow Wilson gave Wilson's opponents additional weapons with which to defeat the League. The objective strength of the book lay in its criticisms of the reparation problem, but one cannot say that Keynes displayed omniscience in all of his economic evaluations and predictions. To the British people, who had achieved all their national war aims at the Paris Peace Conference, political questions may have appeared insignificant; but for France the safety of her eastern frontiers constituted the supreme cause of anxiety and she tended to disregard the economic future of Germany. We have seen already, however, how the consequences of the Ruhr invasion compelled the French to pay heed to the economic realities of Europe; the events of 1923–24 equally forced the British Government to modify its policy. Although the sudden dismay with the peace settlement as far as applied to the Continent of Europe caused the British nation to assume a very critical attitude towards French policy, the official British opposition to the French defense of the peace treaties could never be of a radical nature. Britain, too, wanted to extract reparations from Germany. Moreover, Britain was in no position to police Europe and had to rely on the French army for the protection of the area of the Continent strategically most vital for British security, the Lowlands and northern France. The British Government found it wise in 1922 to offer to France in the place of the abortive Rhine pact of 1919 a guarantee of her eastern frontiers that Lord Curzon called "the outer frontiers" of Britain. Britain felt so safe in these years that the British Foreign Secretary could call the proffered guarantee a gracious "gift" to France, although it did not offer any special British contribution to the maintenance of peace. Not even Anglo-French staff conversations comparable to those held before 1914 were contemplated. The provisions of the Versailles Treaty with regard to the demilitarization of the Rhineland were not altogether forgotten in the draft treaty of 1922, but Lord Curzon told the French ambassador, Count St. Aulaire, that he did not think the British cabinet "would be moved to go in substance at all outside the boundaries of the Treaty of 1919."

In these circumstances the French saw no advantage in the conclusion of the proposed Anglo-French Treaty. They felt certain that in case of a German attack against the French frontiers Britain would be forced to come to the assistance of France, since British self interest, created by geography rather than mere sympathy with France, would compel the British

Government to adopt this course of action. Yet without prior agreement on joint military measures to be employed in such an event, both the Rhine and northern France might be overrun before British intervention could take place. The British army estimates of this period never envisaged the possible need for a British expeditionary force to be sent to the Continent. Small wonder the French were at a complete loss to understand why their political reasoning should be deemed overlogical in Britain.

PEACEMAKING 1919 — A CRITIQUE

HAROLD NICOLSON

Harold Nicolson, eminent writer and diplomat, has given in his *Peacemaking 1919* a classic description of the Paris Peace Conference. Son of Lord Carnock, British career ambassador before World War I, Nicolson himself entered the foreign service in 1909 and in 1919 served as a member of the British peace delegation in Paris. The selection below includes his description of conference routine, as well as his criticisms of the political considerations which in his view triumphed over Wilsonian idealism in the final settlement.

SCENARIO OF THE PEACE CONFERENCE

I T IS not easy, when using the silent machinery of printed words, to reproduce the double stress of turmoil and time-pressure which in Paris constituted the main obstruction to calm thinking or planned procedure: "It was a period of unremitting strain." The sedative notes of such a sentence, as applied to the scurrying cacophony of the Peace Conference, forces one to smile. Only through the medium of a sound film could any accurate impression,

that sense of riot in a parrot house, be conveyed.

Were I to sketch such a scenario of my own impressions, the result would be something as follows. As a recurrent undertone throughout would run the rumble of Time's winged chariot: incessantly reiterant would come the motif of this time pressure — newspapers screaming in headlines against the Dawdlers of Paris, the clamour for demobilisation, "Get the Boys back," the starving millions of Central Europe, the slouching queues of prisoners still behind

From Harold Nicolson, *Peacemaking 1919* (New York, Harcourt, Brace and Company, 1939), New and Cheaper Edition, pp. 152–156, 185–195. Reprinted by permission of Harcourt, Brace and Company.

their barbed wire, the flames of communism flaring, now from Munich, and now from Buda Pesth. Through this recurrent grumble and rumble of the time-motif would pierce the sharper discordances of other sounds; the machine-gun rattle of a million typewriters, the incessant shrilling of telephones, the clatter of motor bicycles, the drone of aeroplanes, the cold voices of interpreters, "le délégué des Etats-Unis constate qu'il ne peut se ranger . . ." the blare of trumpets, the thunder of guns saluting at the Invalides, the rustling of files, a woman in a black woollen shawl singing "Madelon" in front of a café, the crackle of Rolls Royces upon gravel of sumptuous courtyards, and throughout the sound of footsteps hurrying now upon the parquet of some gallery, now upon the stone stairway of some Ministry, and now muffled on the heavy Aubusson of some overheated saloon.

These sound-motifs would be accompanied by a rapid projection of disjointed pictures. The tired and contemptuous eyelids of Clemenceau, the black button-boots of Woodrow Wilson, the rotund and jovial gestures of Mr. Lloyd George's hands, the infinite languor of Mr. Balfour slowly uncrossing his knees, a succession of secretaries and experts bending forward with maps, Foch striding stockily with Weygand hurrying behind. The silver chains of the huissiers at the Quai d'Orsay. Such portraits would be interspersed with files, agenda papers, resolutions, *procès verbaux,* and communiqués. These would succeed each other with extreme rapidity, and from time to time would have to be synchronised and superimposed. "The Plenipotentiaries of the United States of America, of the British Empire, of France, of Italy, and of Japan, of the one part. . . . It is resolved that subject to the approval of the Houses of Congress the President of the United States of America accepts on the behalf of the United States. . . . Si cette frontière était prise en considération, il serait nécessaire de faire la correction indiquée en bleu. Autrement le chemin de fer vers Kaschau serait coupé. . . . These coupons will be accepted in settle-

ment of the table d'hôte meals of the hotel, the whole ticket is to be given up at dinner. . . . M. Venizelos told me last night that he had concluded his agreement with Italy in the following terms: (1) Italy will support Greek claims in Northern Epirus. . . . From the point where the western boundary of the area leaves the Drave in a northerly direction as far as the point about one kilometre to the east of Rosegg (Saint Michael). The course of the Drave downstream. Thence in a north-easterly direction and as far as the western extremity of the Wörthersee, south of Vlelden. A line to be fixed on the ground. The median line of that lake. Thence eastwards to its confluence with the river Glan. The course of the Glanfurt downstream. . . . (1) Audition de M. Dmosky. (2) Rapport de la Commission Interalliée de Teschen. (3) Le rapatriement des troupes du Général Haller. (4) Rapport de M. Hoover. (5) Prisonniers de guerre. (6) Répartition de la marine marchande allemande. . . . From the coming into force of the present Treaty the High Contracting Parties shall renew, in so far as concerns them, and under the reserves indicated in the second paragraph of the present Article, the conventions and arrangements signed at Berne on October 14, 1890, September 20, 1893, July 16, 1895, June 16, 1898, and September 19, 1906, regarding the transportation of goods by rail. If within five years of the coming into force of the present Treaty. . . . Le traité concernent l'entrée de la Bavière dans la confédération de l'Allemagne du Nord, conclu à Versailles le 23 novembre 1870, contient, dans les articles 7 et 8 du protocole final, des dispositions toujours en viguer, reconnaissant. . . . A meeting of the British Empire Delegation will be held on Tuesday the 14th instant at the Villa Majestic at 11.30 a.m. . . . Dr. Nansen came to see me this morning. He represents the urgent necessity of inducing the Supreme Council. . . . An entertainment will be held on Saturday next at 9.30 p.m. in the Ball Room of the Hotel Majestic in aid of the Dockland Settlement. Miss Ruth Draper has kindly consented to give us two

of her well-known character sketches. Tickets may be obtained from the hallporter —
Le Baron Sonnino estimait qu'il y avait lieu d'établir une distinction entre les représentants des Soviets et ceux des autres Gouvernements. Les Alliés combattaient les bolcheviks et les considéraient comme des ennemis. Il n'en était pas de même en ce qui concernait les Finlandais, les Lettons. . . .
Telegram from Vienna. Count Karolyi has resigned and according to telephone message received by Mr. Coolidge this morning from his representative at Buda Pesth communist government has been formed under leadership of Bela Kun. Fate of Allied Missions uncertain. . . . Wir wissen das die Gewalt der deutschen Waffen gebrochen ist. Wir kennen die Macht des Hasses, die uns hier entgegentritt, und wir haben die leidenschaftliche Förderung gehört, dass die Sieger uns zugleich als Ueberwundene zahlen lassen und als Schuldige bestrafen sollen. . . ."

A rapid succession of such captions, accompanied by the whole scale of sound which I have indicated, would furnish a clearer picture of the atmosphere of the Peace Conference than any chronological record in terms of the printed word. Could colour, scent, and touch be added, the picture would be almost complete. The dominant note is black and white, heavy black suits, white cuffs and paper: it is relieved by blue and khaki: the only other colours would be the scarlet damask of the Quai d'Orsay curtains, green baize, pink blotting pads, and the innumerable gilt of the little chairs. For smells you would have petrol, typewriting ribbons, French polish, central heating, and a touch of violet hair-wash. The tactile motifs would be tracing paper, silk, the leather handle of a weighted pouch of papers, the footfeel of very thick carpets alternating with parquet flooring, the stretch of muscle caused by leaning constantly over very large maps, the brittle feel of a cane chair-seat which has been occupied for hours.

And behind it all the ache of exhaustion and despair. . . .

FAILURE

The purpose of this book is, I must repeat, not so much to formulate a record of events, as to catch, before it evaporates, the unhealthy and unhappy atmosphere of the Peace Conference; to convey some of the impression of that gradual drift, away from our early peaks of aspiration towards the low countries where figures laboured hurriedly together in a gathering fog. I apprehend that unless the pressure (the actual inevitability) of this atmosphere is realised as a determining factor in itself, the historian may approach the Conference with wisdom after the event, and may concentrate, in critical tranquility, upon apportioning praise and blame. I do not think however, that any useful description of the Paris Conference can be conveyed in terms of ethical, as distinct from technical, values.

The Conference may, as Mr. Winston Churchill has said, have been a "turbulent collision of embarrassed demagogues." I have already indicated some of the causes which led to turbulence, to collision, and to demagogic methods. Yet in spite of this, many durable, and some useful things were accomplished. Many evil things were avoided. None the less, there were few of us who were not disappointed: and in some of us the Conference inculcated a mood of durable disbelief—a conviction that human nature can, like a glacier, move but an inch or two in every thousand years.

I wish in this concluding chapter to summarise some, at least, of what might be called the psychological factors (or were they symptoms?) of failure; to comment upon the gradual deterioration of our state of mind; to ascribe, if possible, this decline of thought and feeling to some tangible causes. The historian, with every justification will come to the conclusion that we were very stupid men. I think we were. Yet I also think that the factor of stupidity is inseparable from all human affairs. It is too often disregarded as an inevitable concomitant of human behavior; it is too often employed merely as a term of personal affront.

What, in the first place was the nature

of this moral and intellectual deterioration? I can speak with assurance only of my own change of heart, yet I believe that the mutations through which I passed were shared by many others, and that my own loss of idealism coincided with a similar loss of idealism on the part of those (and there were many) who had come to the Conference fired by the same certitudes as myself. Our change of heart can be stated as follows. We came to Paris confident that the new order was about to be established; we left it convinced that the new order had merely fouled the old. We arrived as fervent apprentices in the school of President Wilson: we left as renegades. I wish to suggest, in this chapter (and without bitterness), that this unhappy diminution of standard was very largely the fault (or one might say with greater fairness "the misfortune") of democratic diplomacy.

We arrived determined that a Peace of justice and wisdom should be negotiated: we left it, conscious that the treaties imposed upon our enemies were neither just nor wise. To those who desire to measure for themselves the width of the gulf which sundered intention from practice I should recommend a perusal of the several Notes addressed to the Supreme Council by the German Delegation at Versailles. An excellent summary and confrontation of these Notes is furnished by Professor Hazeltine in Volume II of Temperley's *History of the Peace Conference*. It is impossible to read the German criticism without deriving the impression that the Paris Peace Conference was guilty of disguising an Imperialistic peace under the surplice of Wilsonism, that seldom in the history of man has such vindictiveness cloaked itself in such unctuous sophistry. Hypocrisy was the predominant and unescapable result. Yet was this hypocrisy wholly conscious, wholly deliberate? I do not think so. I certainly agree that the sanctimonious pharisaism of the Treaties is their gravest fault. Yet was there any conscious dissimulation? In some cases (such as the article forbidding Austria to join with Germany) a deliberately evasive form of words was consciously employed. Yet in most cases, hypocrisy *just happened*. How did it happen? The fact that, as the Conference progressed, we were scarcely conscious of our own falsity, may indicate that some deterioration of moral awareness had taken place. We did not realise what we were doing. We did not realise how far we were drifting from our original basis. We were exhausted and overworked. We kept on mumbling our old formulas in the hope that they still bore some relation to our actions. There were few moments when we said to ourselves "This is unjust": there were many moments when we said to ourselves "Better a bad treaty to-day, than a good treaty four months hence." In the dust of controversy, in the rattle of time-pressure we lost all contact with our guiding stars. In interludes the dust would settle, the machine would stop, and we would observe, with tired regret, that these stars were themselves fading pale against the sky. *"Il faut aboutir"* they shouted at us: and we returned to the din and dimness of our compromises. We still desired ardently to maintain our principles intact: it was only in the aftervacancy that we realised that they remained for us only in the form of empty words: it was then, and then only, that we faced the fact that the falsity of our position had led us into being false. It was by then too late.

The above is not written in any desire to defend our state of mind. I am examining only: I am not defending. My contention is that this dimming of our moral awareness constituted the most regrettable and perhaps the only interesting element in our deterioration. I wish to explain how it occurred in the dust of incessant argument, amid the by-paths of unceasing detail, we strayed from the main avenues of our intention: and how it was unconsciously, rather than consciously, that we boasted, on arrival, to have come the way we meant.

The point is, I think, of some importance. If future generations come to believe that the Paris Conference was, in every single point, deliberately and exceptionally hypocritical, they will (when they also come to attend Congresses) be less on their guard against the tired falsity which is inseparable from any attempt to adjust high general principles to low practical detail. In every discussion between sovereign States claiming equality with each other, decisions can only be taken by a unanimous and not a majority vote. This inevitable curse of unanimity leads to the no less inevitable curse of compromise. All compromises have an element of falsity, but when they have to be referred back to governing principles or generalisations a double falsity is introduced. I do not deny the ghastly hypocrisy of the Paris Treaties: I contend only that this hypocrisy was not, in every case, humanly avoidable; and that similar hypocrisy may not, in every case, be humanly avoidable in the future.

It will be contended by any intelligent reader that the above analysis of the nature of our hypocrisy is not, after all, an explanation, but is merely a lame and empty excuse. Yet the explanation is none the less implicit in my argument. It is this. The Paris negotiators were from the very first in a false position. This falsity increased during the whole time that the German Treaty was being discussed. It was the root-cause of the whole failure, of the rapid deterioration in moral awareness. It requires to be analysed into its component parts.

*　　*　　*

I have already indicated in preceding chapters many of the elements of falsity which afflicted the Paris Peace Conference from the start. I have drawn attention to the contradiction between conditions offered at the moment when victory was still uncertain, and the interpretation of those conditions at a moment when triumph, overwhelming and insatiable, was in our hands. I have suggested that an idealism evolved to mitigate the pangs of possible defeat is apt to shift materially when applied to the appetites aroused by actual conquest. I have also indicated the acute difficulty experienced by the negotiators in Paris in reconciling the excited expectations of their own

democracies with the calmer considerations of durable peace-making. Such contrasts can be grouped together under what will forever be the main problem of democratic diplomacy; the problem, that is, of adjusting the emotions of the masses to the thoughts of the rulers. The new diplomacy may be immune to some of the virus of deception which afflicted the old: yet it is acutely sensitive to its own peculiar virus — to the virus of imprecision. What the statesman thinks today, the masses may feel tomorrow. Yet in conditions such as those of the Peace Conference, requiring extreme rapidity of solution, the time-lag between the emotions of the masses and the thoughts of the statesmen is a most disadvantageous factor. The attempt rapidly to bridge the gulf between mass-emotion and expert reason leads, at its worst, to actual falsity, and at its best to grave imprecision. The Paris Peace Conference was not a sample of democratic diplomacy at its best. It was thus by actual falsity that the gulf was bridged.

This general type of falsity, inseparable from all attempts at democratic diplomacy, was in Paris complicated and enhanced by special circumstances which require in their turn to be stated and analysed. The contrast between mass-emotion and expert reason was stated for us in acute and difficult terms. It took the form — the unnecessary and perplexing form — of a contrast not only between the new diplomacy and the old, but between the new world and the old, between Europe and America. I do not say that this contrast was, in all its implications, fully realised at the time. I contend only that it was determinant throughout the whole Conference: that it was, in fact, an unreal and not a real contrast; and that the attempt to reconcile these two unrealities was the essential misconception of the Conference, and the root cause of all resultant falsity. Let me state the contrast in quite simple terms.

On the one hand you had Wilsonism — a doctrine which was very easy to state and very difficult to apply. Mr. Wilson had not invented any new political philosophy, or discovered any doctrine which had not been dreamed of, and appreciated, for many hundred years. The one thing which rendered Wilsonism so passionately interesting at the moment was the fact that this centennial dream was suddenly backed by the overwhelming resources of the strongest Power in the world. Here was a man who represented the greatest physical force which had ever existed and who had pledged himself openly to the most ambitious moral theory which any statesman had ever pronounced. It was not that the ideas of Woodrow Wilson were so apocalyptic: it was that for the first time in history you had a man who possessed, not the desire merely, not the power alone, but the unquestioned opportunity to enforce these ideas upon the whole world. We should have been insensitive indeed had we not been inspired by the magnitude of such an occasion.

On the other hand you had Europe, the product of a wholly different civilisation, the inheritor of unalterable circumstances, the possessor of longer and more practical experience. Through the centuries of conflict the Europeans had come to learn that war is in almost every case contrived with the expectation of victory, and that such an expectation is diminished under a system of balanced forces which renders victory difficult if not uncertain. The defensive value of armaments, strategic frontiers, alliances, and neutralization, could be computed with approximate accuracy: the defensive value of "virtue all round" could not be thus computed. If in fact Wilsonism could be integrally and universally applied, and if in fact Europe could rely upon America for its execution and enforcement, then indeed an alternative was offered infinitely preferable to the dangerous and provocative balances of the European system. Backed by the assurance of America's immediate and unquestioned support, the statesmen of Europe might possibly have jettisoned their old security for the wider security offered them by the theories of Woodrow Wilson. But were they certain that America would

be so unselfish, so almost quixotic, as to make Wilsonism safe for Europe? Were they certain, even that the European Powers would, when it came to the point, apply Wilsonism to themselves? The Fourteen Points were hailed as an admirable method of extracting motes from the eyes of others: would any great and victorious Power apply them for the purposes of extracting beams from their own body politic? The most ardent British advocate of the principle of self-determination found himself sooner or later, in a false position. However fervid might be our indignation regarding Italian claims to Dalmatia and the Dodecanese it could be cooled by a reference, not to Cyprus only, but to Ireland, Egypt, and India. We had accepted a system for others which, when it came to practice, we should refuse to apply to ourselves.

Nor was this the only element of falsity by which the gospel of Woodrow Wilson was discredited from the start. The Anglo-Saxon is gifted with a limitless capacity for excluding his own practical requirements from the application of the idealistic theories which he seeks to impose on others. Not so the Latin. The logical precision of the French, and to a less extent the Italian, genius does not permit such obscurantism. The Anglo-Saxon is apt to accuse the Latin of "cynicism" because he hesitates to adhere to a religion which he would not be prepared to apply to his own conduct as distinct from the conduct of others. The Latin accuses the Anglo-Saxon of "cant" because he desires to enforce upon others a standard of behaviour which he would refuse to adopt himself. The contrast between the two is not, in fact, one between cynicism and hypocrisy, it is one between two divergent habits of mind. The Anglo-Saxon is apt to feel before he thinks, and the Latin is apt to think before he feels. It was this divergence of habit, this gap between reason and emotion, which induced the Latins to examine the Revelation of Woodrow Wilson in a manner more scientific, and therefore more critical, than we did ourselves. From this examination they reached certain deductions which destroyed their faith.

They observed, for instance, that the United States in the course of their short but highly imperialistic history, had constantly proclaimed the highest virtue while as constantly violating their professions and resorting to the grossest materialism. They observed that all Americans liked to feel in terms of Thomas Jefferson but to act in terms of Alexander Hamilton. They observed that such principles as the equality of man were not applied to the yellow man or to the black. They observed that the doctrine of self determination had not been extended either to the Red Indians or even in the Southern States. They were apt to examine "American principles and American tendencies" not in terms of the Philadelphia declaration, but in terms of the Mexican War, of Louisiana, of those innumerable treaties with the Indians which had been violated shamelessly before the ink was dry. They observed that, almost within living memory, the great American Empire had been won by ruthless force. Can we blame them if they doubted, not so much the sincerity as the actual applicability of the gospel of Woodrow Wilson? Can we blame them if they feared lest American realism would, when it came to

the point, reject the responsibility of making American idealism safe for Europe? Can we wonder that they preferred the precisions of their own old system to the vague idealism of a new system which America might refuse to apply even to her own continent?

It is only fair to record that on the American Delegation themselves this unfortunate disparity produced a sense of impotence. The President himself was able to dismiss from his consciousness all considerations which might disturb the foundations of his mystic faith. Colonel House, being a man of robust intelligence, might have been able, had he possessed supreme control, to bridge the gulf in a wholly scientific manner, to evolve an honest triumph of engineering. Yet upon the other members of the delegation, who were ardent and sincere, the suspicion that America was asking Europe to make sacrifices to righteousness which America would never make, and had never made, herself, produced a mood of diffidence, uncertainty, and increasing despair. Had President Wilson been a man of exceptional breadth of vision, of superhuman determination, he might have triumphed over all these difficulties. Unfortunately neither the will-power nor the brain-power of President Wilson were in any sense superhuman.

VERSAILLES TWENTY YEARS
AFTER — A DEFENSE

PAUL BIRDSALL

Of all the problems connected with the peace of Versailles, the figure of Woodrow Wilson looms as the object of the most enduring controversy. From the Fourteen Points to the minutest traits of his personality, Wilson has been intensively subjected to both critical and sympathetic scrutiny. Twenty years after Versailles, at a time when the world was already engulfed in World War II, Professor Paul Birdsall of Williams College completed work on a major review of the Paris peace settlements. Disagreeing sharply with Wilson's critics, Birdsall paid tribute to Wilson and his idealism as well as to the over-all peace settlement which he had so largely inspired.

IF THE FIRST World War taught us anything, it taught us that after four years of bloodshed democracies become thoroughly vindictive toward the enemy who has caused them to suffer. The peoples of England and France were in a mood to "hang the Kaiser" and to "squeeze the orange until the pips squeak." It is by now a commonplace that a hysterical populace in Allied countries called for punishment and destruction of Germany, and Allied leaders, true to the principles of democracy, bowed to the storm. Belief in the unique guilt of the Kaiser for the horrors of the World War was unanimous. Can the peoples of Great Britain and France entertain many doubts about the guilt of Hitler? If they could regard the people of Imperial Germany as "Huns" and barbarians, how will they think of their Nazi enemies?

How can such passions be controlled? They must be controlled if democracy is to solve the problem of a stable peace and of a durable world order. Only in a stable world can democracy survive. Those who decry idealism and justice as sentimental and unrealistic terms in world politics miss the point. For idealism and justice are the very rudiments of common sense. They amount to a practical realization of what the traffic will reasonably bear. They require the sacrifice of immediate vengeance for the sake of long-term enlightened self-interest.

Woodrow Wilson symbolized the forces of reason in the fight for a peace of justice. He spoke too much the language of idealism and self-sacrifice and too little the plain language of a genuine community of interest, and to that extent he brought upon himself the misrepresentation which obscured his real role in the Paris Peace Conference and contributed to the defeat of his program in the United States. A hard-boiled and disillusioned age is quick to gibe about cant and hypocrisy, and Keynes' characterization of the Presbyterian theocrat who was "bamboozled" by Clemenceau and Lloyd George and could not be "debamboozled" has found recent echoes in Harold

From *Versailles Twenty Years After*, copyright, 1941, by Paul Birdsall, pp. 4–9, 295–303. Reprinted by permission of Harcourt, Brace and Company, Inc., and George Allen & Unwin Ltd.

Nicolson's references to the "arid revivalism" of the "American Prophet," in whose pronouncements Nicholson observed "a slight tinge of revivalism, a touch of Methodist arrogance, more than a touch of Presbyterian vanity."

The simple thesis of such writers is that the doctrinaire and unrealistic program of Wilson collapsed under the impact of the power politics of Europe. Nationalist aims triumphed over his principles. There was division of the spoils of war, "bartering about of peoples and provinces from sovereignty to sovereignty as if they were chattels or pawns in a game," in defiance of his principles of self-determination. Worst of all, there had to be pretense. The Allied governments had accepted Wilson's program. While violating it, still they must pay it lip-service and hence, according to Keynes, they joined with Wilson in weaving "that web of sophistry and Jesuitical exegesis that was finally to clothe with insincerity the language and substance of the whole Treaty." Keynes in his disillusionment has fixed the legend of a Carthaginian Peace in Wilsonian disguise.

This is caricature, not history, but like most successful caricature it has enough verisimilitude to be plausible. Scarcely as much can be said for Lloyd George's recent *Apologia,* which presents the exactly opposite thesis that Versailles was a purely Wilsonian peace. Only he does not call it Wilsonian, because it was he, Lloyd George himself, who achieved the peace of justice practically single-handed. Always adept at sleight of hand, in his latest masterpiece he demonstrates that he achieved Wilson's program in spite of Wilson. Like most commentators, he deplores the choice of war-worn Paris as the seat of the Peace Conference, but hastily adds, "I cannot point out that in the sequel the purely Parisian influence made any serious impression on the actual stipulations of the document finally agreed to, *since I cannot discover a single particular in which it has departed from the terms of peace laid down by the Allies before the War came to an end.*" That statement

acquires a peculiarly fine flavor of irony from the fact that Lloyd George himself bears major responsibility for the most egregious breach of faith contained in the entire treaty. The "Reparation" chapter of the Treaty of Versailles, besides being a clear violation of the Pre-Armistice Agreement with Germany, proved in the outcome to be the most disastrous section of the treaty. Keynes spoke with authority and even with clairvoyance on that subject.

The prosaic truth is that elements of good and bad were combined in the treaties. There were Carthaginian features like the Reparation settlement and Wilsonian features like the League of Nations. There was actually a distribution of colonial spoils of war, but only after the valuable principle had been established that colonial powers administered their new estates under specified conditions and subject to review and correction by an international tribunal, the League of Nations. The territorial settlement in Europe was by no means the wholesale, iniquitous, and cynical perversion of Wilson's principles of self-determination which has been pictured.

Harold Nicolson has explained many of the worst boundary decisions as resulting from sheer lack of coordination between the various expert commissions charged with a supremely difficult task. Yet most critics of the settlement forget the difficulties of that task. One of the commonest criticisms is directed against the shattering of the former Dual Monarchy of Austria-Hungary into those fragments called the Succession States. In this view the negotiators at Paris should have foreseen the economic and political need of a Danubian Confederation to combine the fragments. Yet Austria-Hungary had fallen apart before the Peace Conference convened and *de facto* national governments ruled the pieces. British and American delegates in Paris actually proposed a customs union for the area, only to encounter Italian objection, based on the principle of "divide and rule."

The populations of central Europe are hopelessly mixed, and therefore Simon-pure self-determination is impossible. Any boundary will leave national minorities on one side or the other. Moreover, the history of the past few years has certainly justified the commissioners in taking account of strategic factors in the award of boundaries to the new states of Europe. The aftermath of the Munich settlement proved that Czechoslovakia could not exist without possession of its historic and strategic boundaries in the Bohemian mountains, even if that area is inhabited by 3,000,000 Germans. It is equally clear that a special status for the purely German city of Danzig, involving segregation from the political structure of the German Reich, is essential to the security of the Polish Corridor, which on the basis of pre-war German statistics is "indisputably" Polish territory. Hitler's demand for the reincorporation of Danzig in the German Reich was accompanied by a demand for territory across the Corridor itself. To have granted the demand for Danzig would have left the way open for the "fourth and final partition of Poland," even without the formality of war. If the Allies should ever conquer Germany again, the negotiators of the new Versailles will face precisely the same dilemma. They can simply accept the traditional German thesis that Slavic peoples as an inferior racial breed have no right to independent national existence and permit Germany to rule Poland, Bohemia, Moravia, and Slovakia, or, if they acknowledge any right of self-determination of these peoples, they must inevitably violate in some degree the rights of German minorities. Hard as it is to visualize in 1941, it would not be surprising if the negotiators of the new Versailles were to recreate Poland and Czechoslovakia within something like the original Versailles boundaries.

In any case, it is well to be reminded by Professor Seton-Watson that it was not directly the Great Powers which profited from the partition of former German and Austro-Hungarian territory, but those new Slavic states which had themselves been partitioned and dominated for centuries. If their sense of injury was deep and their territorial appetite greedy in 1919, those sentiments are not likely to be extinguished by their present plight. If they received an unduly large measure of sympathy from the victorious Great Powers at that time, they would again secure at least their due share.

Finally, the territorial settlement contained in the various treaties negotiated at Paris is still, with all its faults, the closest approximation to an ethnographic map of Europe that has ever been achieved. If the next Peace Conference does better, it will be because of the achievements as well as the mistakes of Versailles. It can scarcely hope to do better unless some leading figure is prepared to undertake the role of Woodrow Wilson in restraining the forces of extravagant nationalism. It will take a brave man to assume that role.

* * *

The treaty was essentially a compromise between Anglo-American and French conceptions of a stable international order. On the one hand, immediate French concern for military security was taken care of by the limitation of German armaments, demilitarization of the Rhineland area and Allied military occupation for a fifteen-year period, and — finally — an Anglo-American treaty of military guarantee. These were certainly adequate guarantees, granted the full weight of English and American resources to support them, and there could be every hope that they would enlist France in the cause of an effective League of Nations. They represented the minimum price which English and American negotiators had to pay for French abandonment of their traditional policy of entirely dismembering Germany. They were a realistic concession to French needs without violating the Fourteen Points in any important particular. Above all, they were regarded as essentially interim measures to provide the necessary breathing spell for the consolidation of the League. Military occupation of German soil would end in fifteen years, at the very moment when residents of the Saar valley might vote to return to German sovereignty; German disarmament was to be the prelude to general disarmament; and the Anglo-American treaty of military guarantee was to cease when the League itself was thought strong enough to provide general security.

The Reparation settlement was the chief stumbling block, partly because of impossible financial demands, even more because it combined an egregious breach of faith with an impolitic accusation of moral turpitude. In both financial and political results it proved disastrous. Yet, even here, American participation in the settlement could be counted upon to exert a moderating influence, while the English were certain to recover their sanity on a subject so close to their own interest, and would try to undo the harm they had done by their original collaboration with the French to defeat the American program. The Reparation issue emphasized more than any other the necessity of continuing Anglo-American cooperation to make effective Anglo-American conceptions of a world order.

It is vitally important to distinguish between the treaty as a written constitution and as a policy in action. Students of constitutional law have long since learned to distinguish between the intentions of founding fathers, as expressed in the verbal niceties of a constitutional document on the one hand, and the practical application of organic law to a constantly changing society on the other hand. Students of international politics, more particularly students of international law, have on the whole been less discriminating. The history of the Treaty of Versailles would have been very different if the United States had ratified it, since the treaty itself was largely shaped on the assumption that it would have behind it both the authority of the United States and the impartial influence of the United States as a constantly moderating influence in its enforcement.

The defection of the United States destroyed the Anglo-American preponderance which alone could have stabilized Europe. It impaired the authority and prestige of the League at its birth and it precipitated an Anglo-French duel which reduced Europe to the chaos from which Hitler emerged to produce new chaos which he has christened the "New Europe." Practically and immediately, it destroyed the Anglo-American treaty of military guarantee which was to have been one of the main props of French security, and it removed every prospect of material American support for all the other guarantees of French security. The French had very reluctantly yielded their extreme program for the dismemberment of Germany in return for guarantees which were now to appear worthless. Here was complete confirmation of the French military logic which had always been skeptical of Anglo-American sentimentalism, professions of faith, and reliance on the voluntary principle. Clemenceau did not long survive, politically, his concessions to Anglo-American blandishments, and a reactionary nationalist like Poincaré, who had intrigued in 1919 to prevent those concessions, was more than likely to revive traditional French military projects in a dangerous form.

English sentiment was already developing the guilt-complex about the whole Treaty of Versailles which, among other factors, paralyzed English foreign policy from Versailles to Munich. It would be interesting to speculate as to how much that guilt-complex was the result of the brilliant writing of John Maynard Keynes. Devastatingly accurate and prophetic in its analysis of the economic aspects of the treaty, his *The Economic Consequences of the Peace* included the whole treaty in one sweeping condemnation as a "Carthaginian Peace," and his caricatures of the leading negotiators at Paris immediately fixed stereotypes which still affect much of the writing about the Paris Peace Conference. At the very time that the United States Government repudiated the Versailles settlement legally, the English people did so morally, and the French Government saw all the guarantees of the settlement doubly impaired. *Perfide Albion* became the popular text for French commentary on European affairs in the early post-war years.

The weak and necessarily opportunist German Republic, itself the artificial creation of President Wilson's pre-armistice notes, was quick to observe the divergence and to capitalize on the opportunity offered for evasion. The French naturally attributed their difficulties with Germany to English bad faith, and the more England displayed sympathy for Germany, the more the French tended to resort to reactionary, violent, and military measures of very doubtful legality under the terms of the treaty. The greater the ruthlessness of French efforts to enforce the treaty on an evasive Germany, the more sympathy was available for Germany in England, and in the United States.

No one of the three Powers involved in this contest was strong enough to make its will and its policy prevail to break the vicious circle of conflict. English sympathy was sufficient to encourage German resistance, but official British policy was not strong enough to prevent the retaliatory measures taken by the French Government. France, single-handed, was strong enough to impose punitive and destructive measures on Germany, but not sufficiently strong to effect a lasting settlement, while Germany was strong enough to resist complete capitulation only at the cost of measures ultimately destructive of German economy and political stability.

Reparation demands were the focal point of the struggle and they proved the nemesis for Lloyd George's behavior at the Peace Conference. Here, the French had a strong legal case based on provisions which the English themselves had helped to write into the treaty over the objections of the American Delegation. English enlightenment came too late to alter the treaty legally and, consequently, British exhortations to the French for greater reasonableness looked like characteristic betrayal and a breach of contract. French leaders felt that both Great Britain and the United States had betrayed the Versailles provisions for French security and felt entitled to use undoubted legal rights to reparation as the means of gaining security in their own way.

Poincaré secured a verdict from the Reparation Commission — over the protest of the British representative that Germany was in default on her reparation payments and, in conjunction with Belgium, ordered a military occupation of the Ruhr valley on the right bank of the Rhine. Law Officers of the British Crown vainly pronounced the action illegal under the terms of the treaty; the British Government could do nothing to prevent it. Although Poincaré justified the occupation as legitimate application of treaty sanctions merely to secure the economic resources to which France was legally entitled — "Productive Guarantees" was the phrase he used — the occupation soon became the cover for familiar French military intrigue to dismember Germany. Again the entire Rhineland area seethed with "Separatist" activity of the sort which Clemenceau had stopped in 1919 as the result of President Wilson's protests.

French action was a failure in both its economic and its political aspects. It encountered the passive resistance of the German workers in the Ruhr and could not capitalize on its physical control of German resources, while the Separatist movement as a purely artificial creation of French generals could not survive the spotlight of publicity which the English Government was able to throw upon it as the result of investigations by their Munich consul, Mr. Clive. Meantime, the costs of occupation in connection with the collapse of German economy had reacted violently on the French financial structure. The reactionary nationalist Poincaré fell from office and was replaced by Herriot, internationalist by party doctrine and by conviction, at the same time that Ramsay MacDonald became the first Labor Prime Minister of Great Britain. The Anglo-French duel was temporarily at an end. Was it too late?

Germany, too, had produced a realistic and moderate leader in Stresemann, who would cooperate with his French and British colleagues to stabilize Europe, provided economic resources could be found to heal the financial and psychological wounds of both the war and the peace. Today it can be seen that the German wounds were fatal. Although in an immediate sense they were self-inflicted and warrant the technical verdict of suicide, neither psychiatrist nor historian can be content with a coroner's verdict and would want to know something of the circumstances which drove the victim to desperation. The weak German Republic fell heir to a currency already inflated by the strain of war economy and reparation liabilities, which could be bolstered only by drastic taxation, and the incidence of that taxation would affect those elements of the population most hostile to the republic and most bitter against the peace treaty.

The German Government was between the upper and nether millstones of impossible reparation demands and the intransigence of the only people within Germany who could afford to make any effort to pay them. Under the circumstances, it employed the printing presses to create money which gave immediate relief to both government and industry from their bonded debt, by decreasing the value of the currency with which they paid it. Such a course inevitably led to default on reparation payments, but in any case that was probably inevitable in the long run, and in view of the British attitude there was a reasonably good chance that default would escape punishment.

It is likely that one object of the French occupation of the Ruhr valley was to break the resistance of the large industrialists by seizure of the citadel of their strength. In that object, as in all others, French policy was a failure. It was not the Ruhr industry, but the already hard-pressed German Government, which bore the cost of subsidizing the German workers of the Ruhr in passive resistance to French exploitation. In default of taxes on industry to support the cost, the Government once more had

recourse to the printing presses. To cheat the French, it destroyed the value of the German mark and, with it, the economic position of the most stable element in German politics — the German middle class. While the large industrialist was being freed of the remainder of his bonded debt, it was at the expense of his creditors, the investors, and of all people who lived on fixed income or salary.

The balance of political power almost inevitably shifted from the impoverished middle groups — which were potentially the most loyal supporters of the German Republic — toward the industrialist element whose Republican sentiments were, at best, lukewarm. Nor was it merely that a formerly important class had lost both its economic and its political position. It did not, thereby, become negligible, passive, impotent. It developed a positive hostility to the institutions which had betrayed them. It became a productive recruiting ground for Hitler's Nazi movement. The very foundations for republican and democratic institutions in Germany were thus permanently impaired as a consequence of the Reparation Settlement, American defection from the whole Peace Settlement, and the Anglo-French duel culminating in the occupation of the Ruhr.

Stresemann was the only German leader with sufficient realism and force to secure support from his erstwhile colleagues among the industrialist group, in his efforts to stabilize the Republic and to institute a policy of genuine collaboration with Great Britain and France in stabilizing Europe. The era of Locarno suffused the international scene with an unreal glow which hid the fatal lesions in the European body politic. The two essentials for a genuine stabilization were lacking. The deep fissures in the economic foundations of Europe had been merely papered over with American loans, and, as Stresemann complained shortly before his death, the political concessions which British and French leaders were willing to offer him had always been too little and too late to popularize his régime and his policy within Germany; too late to win German youth for the cause of peace.

With the world-wide economic collapse, Germans increasingly accepted Hitler's thesis that the victors of 1919 would yield only to force and never to reason, and the policy of "appeasement" adopted by Britain and France fortified their faith. Voluntary appeasement of Stresemann's Germany — the Germany of the Weimar Republic — could have been largely confined to the economic sphere and could have won German support to other major provisions of the Treaty of Versailles.

Only too late did British and French leaders observe that Hitler was less concerned about rectification of the "injustices" of the *Diktat* of Versailles than with the conquest of Europe. The muddle and confusion in liberal and democratic communities about the real character of Versailles contributed to the stupidity of Allied policy from Versailles to Armageddon.

THE CASE FOR FRANCE

ANDRÉ TARDIEU

André Tardieu, who in 1929–1930 and again in 1932 became Premier of France, was one of the principal framers of the political and territorial clauses of the Treaty of Versailles. He was also president of the Council of Five which in June 1919 drew up the Allied reply to the German observations on the draft treaty. An intimate associate of Clemenceau, Tardieu was one of the most effective spokesmen for the French case and became, after 1919, a leading defender of the settlement. The selection below includes excerpts from official French conference memoranda personally drawn up by Tardieu.

THE WORK which awaited the framers of the Peace was as great and as unprecedented as the war which was to be brought to a close.

Great and unprecedented in its scope: for the first time in history entire nations had fought. Seventy million men had been mobilized, thirty million had been wounded and nearly ten million had died. Nothing in the past could compare with it. The dead alone outnumbered all the Armies of Napoleon. Great and unprecedented in its complexity: nation having fought nation, there had been brought into play the sum total of all national forces: agricultural, industrial, commercial, and financial. All these potent factors of international life had to be taken into account in making the Treaty. Read over the great peace treaties of the past — for the most part child's play compared to this! Frontier changes limited to a few fragments of the map of Europe; indemnities of a few millions — the five thousand millions exacted in 1871 from France were looked upon at the time as a financial monstrosity and a gross abuse of power; economic clauses in which the victor imposed upon the vanquished the most

From André Tardieu, *The Truth About the Treaty* (Indianapolis, 1921), pp. 77–80, 114–123, 147–148, 163–167. Reprinted by permission of the Bobbs-Merrill Company.

favoured nation clause! A peace treaty had certain classic outlines which were filled in according to more or less settled traditions.

The map of the world had to be remade, and under what conditions! Germany's persistent savagery had left more ruins in the victorious countries than the invasions of the barbarians had ever made in the lands they overran and conquered. The resources of all the belligerents had been equally exhausted by the duration of the struggle, and as the damages rightly demanded by the creditors rose, the capacity for payment of the debtors fell. Mr. Lloyd George had said in 1918, "Germany shall pay for everything." When the Conference met, it was of necessity obliged to ascertain how much and in what manner Germany could pay. And ways had to be devised to extend the time of payment; for it was quite evident a country no matter how rich could not pay hundreds of millions in a few months and no matter how criminal could not have undergone so prolonged a strain without diminishing its resources. The execution of the peace terms thus became not a matter of months but of years. It implied a lasting union of the forces which had won the war. Not the victors alone but the whole world had to be given the certainty that Germany would not repeat her offense. The fundamental aims of Liberty and Justice which for fifty-two months had furnished the moral strength and stimulus of the nations in arms had to be realized. Finally the unity of the Allies which had led to their victory had to be maintained and made closer so that they might be as well prepared for common action in the future as they had been in the past. Failing this, the Peace would be lacking in the essential factor that had won the Victory.

The history of the war foreshadowed the nature of the Peace as much by the official acts of Governments as by the spontaneous expression of public opinion. When France knew that she was being attacked by Germany, she proclaimed her war aims with a single voice. They were the defense of her frontiers, the redemption of Alsace-Lorraine and the maintenance of national liberty as opposed to a policy of aggression and domination. In the Parliament and in the Press there was not a discordant note. France had bought this unanimity, the essential condition of success, with forty-three years of anguish. It was the memory of those dark days which gave substance to France's conception of Peace and War. Attacked once more France was once more going to fight for Right. Such is our entry into the war — now for the other nations. Serbia, having made every possible concession, cannot tolerate the substitution of another Power for her own on her own soil. Russia refusing to renounce the Slav gospel by abandoning Serbia to Austria's extortion. Belgium spurning the cynical offer to betray her word and her friends. Great Britain too, accepting the challenge to keep faith with a "scrap of paper." Group these facts, link them to the past, compare them with Germany's aggression and her methods, "Necessity knows no law." It is a conflct between two opposing principles. On one side the nations who put their faith in Might, on the other those who believe in Right. On one side the peoples who seek to enslave, on the other the free peoples who, whether they defend themselves against aggression or whether they come to the assistance of those attacked, are ready to sacrifice their lives to remain independent, masters of their own affairs at home and of their destinies abroad.

The war lasted and grew greater. Each passing hour emphasized and confirmed its original character. In 1915 Italy joins the Allies after laying down the conditions on which she leaves the Triple Alliance. Why? Because from Trentino to Trieste she has heard the voices of the *irredenti* calling. In 1916 Roumania comes in. Why? Because from beyond the plains of Transylvania the lament of Magyarized Roumanians had crossed the Carpathian Mountains. In 1917, Greece comes in. Why? Because on the borders of Macedonia, of Thrace and of Asia Minor she had felt — despite the German leanings of her King — the soul of ancient Hellas stirring. The breath of liberty passes everywhere. For a half century Alsace Lorraine had been the symbol and the flaming torch of the oppressed. From East to West all who believed in the liberation of the oppressed and in the right of peoples to self-determination rallied to the echoes of the Marne and of Verdun. As time passed the circle of our supporters widened. And then came the democracy of the United States. When she entered the struggle, her war aims were indefinite but in a few weeks she too understood and had a clear conception of what she was fighting for. From the Atlantic to the Pacific the word went forth. We are going to fight in Europe. Against what? Against Autocracy and Militarism. For what? For Justice and the Liberty of Nations. Words, mere words, answer the "realists." Yes, mere words, but words for which millions of soldiers stand ready to die. Words which are a living force. Words which from France have spread to the new world and have mobilized the hearts of the people without which there can be no military mobilization in a democracy. We are fighting for our ideal and for our frontier. America had no frontier to defend but she adopted our ideal and made it hers.

That is why — be it pleasing or not, a cause for congratulation or regret — the war of 1914 had a meaning and an aim of its own before any Government had made a declaration. From the first day of the German aggression, it was a war of peoples and of nationalities. A war for popular and national rights. Such it remained to the very end. That was why, in the closing months, Polish, Czecho-Slovakian and Croatian regiments sprang from the soil. That is why millions of men made the last great sacrifice. That is why the Peace was to be the peace of free nations, of nations liberated from the forces of oppression. The peoples had spoken. The Governments in Europe and in America did but register their will. All declarations of "war aims" — invariably and identically — reflected the clear convictions and simple principles which led the Armies into battle.

* * *

Thus time passed, from the end of December, 1918, to the beginning of July, 1919. A time of complexities and of difficulties, a time of overwhelming work and responsibility but also of inspiring effort and result; a time often dramatic. I have explained the inner workings of the machine. I shall now attempt to show the extent of its output.

Something of the wild exhilaration of the Armistice which soon sobered down into a tranquil optimism had marked the first meeting of the Conference. Excessive optimism prevailed as to agreement on the application of principles; excessive optimism prevailed as to the power of this imposing group of victors to control the actual course of events. I have told how France proposed a programme of work which had been rejected as too hard-and-fast and systematic. The Anglo-Saxons preferred to deal with the most pressing matters first. So the Russian question was taken up, with what naïve hopes later events have shown. Then there was the hopeless failure of Prinkipo, vainly prophesied from the first by M. Clemenceau. Then — all the while attempting to disarm Germany and to draw up the pact of the League of Nations — we began to hold meetings for information. Interminable statements, many of which revealed an alarming Imperialism on the part of the most recent beneficiaries of victory, were listened to without discussion. About this time the United States and Great Britain both calling for the presence of the heads of their respective Governments, Mr. Wilson and Mr. Lloyd George had to go away. Five days later, M. Clemenceau was struck down by an assassin and had to retire temporarily with a bullet in his lung. It was a fallow and discouraging time, a time of difficulties and of vain disputes over questions of procedure — modified Armistice, preliminary terms of Peace or Treaty. However, inside progress was being made.

The commissions were filing their reports in quick succession. By the end of March, their work was about completed. It was at this moment that the Council of Four which met for the first time on March 24, took up this material. In six weeks of continuous effort, they were going to clear away the underbrush, lay the foundations and build up the Treaty.

Then discussions began. Calm and unruffled on most points, bitter and stormy on three of the most important to France: the left bank of the Rhine, the Sarre Valley and the question of reparations. These three points took up long sittings and led to fierce debates. Furthermore on certain occasions two tendencies began to appear which foreshadowed future difficulties. France, usually supported by the United States, demanded that the accepted principles of the Peace be unwaveringly applied: restitutions, reparations, guarantees.

"We were attacked," said M. Clemenceau, "we are victorious. We represent right, and might is ours. This might must be used in the service of the right."

Mr. Lloyd George did not say no. Indeed, he sometimes urged exemplary severity, as for the punishment of the Kaiser and his accomplices or to force payment of the expenses of the war. But at times also his parliamentary obsession would come over him. Under the influence of some of his assistants — such as General Smuts — or after breakfasting with some Labour Leader, he would arrive at the meeting looking glum, and announce, "They will not sign." That was his great anxiety. It led him to write long Notes in which he laid down for himself and recommended to his allies a policy of extreme moderation.

"We must have," he kept repeating, "a German Government that will sign. The one now in power is but a shadow. If our terms are too severe it will fall. And then look out for Bolshevism."

At the end of March this obsession became so threatening to the most vital clauses of the Treaty that M. Clemenceau felt called upon to meet it with uncompromis-ing directness which Anglo-Saxons accept, because they consider it fair and which impresses them far more than shifting resistance. On his instructions I drew up a Note in which Mr. Lloyd George's point of view was refuted step by step. It read:

March 31st

I

The French Government is in complete accord with the general aim of Mr. Lloyd George's Note to make a lasting Peace and for that a just Peace.

It does not believe on the other hand that this principle, which is its own, really leads to the conclusions deduced from it in this Note.

II

This Note suggests granting moderate territorial conditions to Germany in Europe in order not to leave her after the Peace with feelings of deep resentment.

This method would be of value if the last war had merely been for Germany an European war, but this is not the case.

Germany before the war was a great world power whose "future was on the water." It was in this world power that she took pride. It is this world power that she will not console herself for having lost.

Now we have taken away from her — or we are going to take away from her — without being deterred by the fear of her resentment — all her Colonies, all her Navy, a great part of her merchant Marine (on account of Reparations), her foreign markets in which she was supreme.

Thus we are dealing her the blow which she will feel the worst and it is hoped to soften it by some improvement in territorial terms. This is a pure illusion, the remedy is not adequate to the ill.

If for reasons of general policy, it is desired to give certain satisfactions to Germany, it is not in Europe that they must be sought. This kind of appeasement will be vain so long as Germany is cut off from world politics.

In order to appease Germany (if such is the desire) we must offer her colonial satisfactions, naval satisfactions, satisfactions of commercial expansion. But the Note of March 26 merely contemplates giving her European territorial satisfactions.

III

Mr. Lloyd George's Note fears that if the territorial conditions imposed on Germany are too severe, it will give an impetus to Bolshevism. Is it not to be feared that this would be precisely the result of the action suggested?

The Conference has decided to call to life a certain number of new States. Can it without committing an injustice sacrifice them out of regard for Germany by imposing upon them inacceptable frontiers? If these peoples — notably Poland and Bohemia — have so far resisted Bolshevism, they have done so by the development of national spirit. If we do violence to this sentiment, they will become the prey of Bolshevism and the only barrier now existing between Russian Bolshevism and German Bolshevism will be broken down.

The result will be either a Confederation of Central and Eastern Europe under the leadership of Bolshevist Germany or the enslavement of this same vast territory by Germany swung back to reaction after a period of general anarchy. In either case, the Allies will have lost the war.

The policy of the French Government is on the contrary to give strong support to these young nations with the help of all that is liberal in Europe and not to seek at their expense to attenuate — which besides would be useless — the colonial, naval and commercial disaster which the Peace inflicts on Germany.

If in order to give to these young nations frontiers which are essential to their national life, it is necessary to transfer to their sovereignty Germans, the sons of those who enslaved them, one may regret having to do this and do it only with measure, but it cannot be avoided.

Moreover, by depriving Germany totally and definitely of her colonies because she has ill-treated the natives, one forfeits the right to refuse to Poland or to Bohemia their natural frontiers on the ground that Germans have occupied their territory as the fore-runners of Pan-Germanism.

IV

The Note of March 26 insists — and the French Government is in complete agreement — on the necessity of making a Peace that will appear to Germany to be a just Peace.

But it may be remarked that taking German mentality into consideration, it is not sure that the Germans will have the same idea of what is just as the Allies have.

Finally it must be retained that this impression of justice must be felt not only by the enemy but also, and first of all, by the Allies. The Allies who have fought together must conclude a Peace which will be fair to all of them.

But what would be the result of following the method suggested in the Note of March 26?

A certain number of full and final guarantees would be ensured to the maritime nations which have never been invaded.

Full and final cession of the German colonies.

Full and final surrender of the German Navy.

Full and final surrender of a large part of the German merchant Marine.

Full and lasting, if not final, exclusion of Germany from foreign markets.

To the continental nations, however, that is to say to those who have suffered the most from the war, only partial and deferred solutions are offered.

Partial solutions such as the reduced frontier suggested for Poland and Bohemia.

Deferred solutions such as the defensive undertaking offered to France for the protection of her territory.

Deferred solutions such as the proposed arrangement for the Sarre coal.

There is here an inequality which may well have a disastrous influence on the after-war relations between the Allies, which are more important than the after-war relations between Germany and the Allies.

It has been shown in Paragraph I that it would be an illusion to hope to find in territorial satisfactions given to Germany a sufficient compensation for the world-wide disaster she has sustained. May it be permitted to add that it would be an injustice to make the weight of these compensations fall upon those of the Allied nations which have borne the brunt of the war.

These countries cannot bear the costs of the Peace after having borne the cost of the war. It is essential that they too shall have the feeling that the Peace is just and equal for all.

Failing this, it is not only Central Europe in which Bolshevism may be feared, for as events have shown, no atmosphere is more favourable to Bolshevism than that of national disappointment.

V

The French Government desires to confine itself for the time being to these considerations of general policy.

It pays full homage to the intentions which inspire Mr. Lloyd George's Note, but it believes that the considerations which the present Note deduces from it are in accord with justice and the general interest.

It is by these considerations that the French Government will be guided in the coming exchange of views during the discussion of the terms suggested by the Prime Minister of Great Britain.

Mr. Lloyd George is ardent; but he has a good heart and a keen sense of justice. After a few hard words — face to face — the distance between the two points of view grew less and that of France made headway. The problem of the Sarre was the first to be solved early in April with the cordial assistance of the British Prime Minister. That of the left bank of the Rhine was solved on April 22, despite his repeated objections. The agreement on reparations was reached at about the same time and on the evening of May 6 the text of the Treaty was delivered by the printers. Thanks to steps taken by France, the name of Italy appeared upon it although news of the return of her plenipotentiaries had been received only the night before. On the seventh afternoon the terms of peace were solemnly handed to Count von Brockdorff-Rantzau. The German made a cold, harsh, and insolent speech. As we were leaving Mr. Lloyd George, exasperated, said to me:

"It is hard to have won the war and to have to listen to that."

A few days passed and the German counter-proposals began to come in. The first received were met almost without discussion by negative replies couched in firm and determined language. Already the Austrian Treaty was being taken up. It looked as though everything was settled with Germany once and for all.

As a matter of fact, the second and most serious crisis of the Conference was at hand. It lasted from May 25 to June 16.

The British Cabinet held two meetings in the last week of May which renewed and redoubled all the fears which the Prime Minister had felt in March. These fears were not as a matter of fact confined to him alone. Even in France many who have since become uncompromising then favoured concessions. Men repeated "Will they sign?" And some suggested a general back-down in order to induce them to sign. Those were atrocious days. Mr. Lloyd George, thoroughly alarmed by the consequences either of a refusal to sign or of a crisis in Germany, suggested unthinkable concessions on almost every point. He excused himself for doing it so tardily. He spoke of consulting the Commons. The work of two months was threatened with ruin. M. Clemenceau stood firm. If there was to be a break, he would go before the French Chamber and resign.

"We know the Germans better than you," he declared, "our concessions will only encourage their resistance while depriving our own peoples of their rights. We do not have to beg pardon for our victory."

President Wilson did not demand any change in the political clauses of the Peace and did not insist on the changes in the financial clauses which were suggested by his experts. Nevertheless no final decision was taken. Oppressive hours; exhausting sittings from which men emerged broken. On June 10 to force the issue I addressed to Mr. House the following letter which he showed the same evening to President Wilson:

June 10, 1919

My dear friend,

Very grave mistakes have been made during the past week: there is only just time to repair them.

For more than five months the heads of Governments and their experts have studied the terms of the Peace to be imposed on Germany. They have reached an agreement and they have communicated to the Germans a text which, if it does not yet bind Count Brockdorff — in any case unquestionably binds the Allies.

Could the Allies suppose that this text would be satisfactory to Germany? Of course not. However, they adopted it. Germany protests, as it was certain she would. Immediately a modification of the text is undertaken. I say this is a confession of weakness and a confession of lack of seriousness, for which all the Allied Governments will pay dearly in terms of public opinion! Is it an impossible Treaty? Is it an unjust Treaty? Count Brockdorff believes that it is. If we change it, we admit that we think as he does. What a condemnation of the work we have done during the past sixteen weeks!

Mr. Lloyd George has said, "But they will not sign and we shall have a thousand difficulties." It is the argument we heard so often during the war—after the battle of the Marne, after Verdun, after the German offensive in the spring of 1918, people said in all of our countries, "Let us make peace to avoid difficulties." We did not listen to them and we did well. We went on with the war and we won it. Shall we have less heart for peace than we had for war?

I add that these public discussions between Allies over a Treaty drawn up between Allies weaken us more every day in the eyes of an adversary who respects only firmness (see the reports from Versailles which arrived to-day).

Thus on the general principle my opinion is this: a week ago, we ought to have answered the Germans, "We will change nothing." If we had only made this answer, the Treaty would be signed to-day. We did not do it. What ought we do now?

As regards the special principles about which amendments are being considered, what is the position?

Reparations? The British who made the first suggestion of amendment are with us to-day against any modification and it is your delegation which proposes (along with other changes which France cannot possibly accept), a total figure of 125 thousand million francs which would barely cover as far as France is concerned the two-thirds of the specific damages, reparation for which is imposed on Germany by a text of May 7. We will not accept it.

League of Nations? We have laid down after four months of study the conditions in which Germany may enter the League. Are we going to change them? Are we going to confess that our decision falls before the

observations of Count Brockdorff? How after that could we defend the Treaty before our respective Parliaments?

All these vacillations, which were repeated in the matters of the Sarre and of the left bank of the Rhine, were the results of the initial mistake. But let me add another word.

No one has the right to ask France to accept such terms. France has an unique experience of Germany. No one has suffered as she has. It is useless to think of persuading France to accept such close cohabitation with Germany in the near future in violation of the text of the Covenant, first of all because France will not accept it and then because it is not just.

When the question arose of giving a hearing to the Irish, every one gave way to the British objections. When the question arose of Japan's status in the League of Nations, every one gave way to the American objections. When dealing with Germany it is France that must be heard.

But above all I would not have the moral position of the Allies sacrificed to the Brockdorff memorandum. I would not have them subjected to the unjustifiable humiliation of admitting that the peace built up by them after more than four months of incessant labour is, as Germany asserts, an unjust and impossible peace, for this is contrary to the truth.

Signed: André Tardieu.

Towards the end of June the atmosphere began to clear. Reason—represented by France—resumed her rights. The amendments suggested a fortnight before gradually vanished one by one. On the sixteenth the Allied answer to the German Notes was handed to Count Brockdorff. Drawn up by Mr. Lloyd George's own secretary—Mr. Philip Kerr—it was on every essential point the eloquent expression of the ideals which France had upheld for five months. I will cite only its more salient passages:

In the view of the Allied and Associated Powers the war which began on August 1, 1914, was the greatest crime against humanity and the freedom of peoples that any nation calling itself civilized has ever consciously committed. . . .

Germany's responsibility, however, is not confined to having planned and started the war. She is no less responsible for the savage and inhuman manner in which it was conducted. . . .

The conduct of Germany is almost unexampled in human history. The terrible responsibility which lies at her door can be seen in the fact that no less than seven million dead lie buried in Europe while more than twenty million others carry upon them the evidence of wounds and suffering because Germany saw fit to gratify her lust for tyranny by resort to war.

The Allied and Associated Nations believe that they will be false to those who have given their all to save the freedom of the world if they consent to treat this war on any other basis than as a crime against humanity and right. . . .

Justice, therefore, is the only possible basis for the settlement of the accounts of this terrible war. Justice is what the German delegation asks for and what Germany has been promised. Justice is what Germany shall have. But it must be Justice for all. There must be Justice for the dead and wounded and for those who have been orphaned and bereaved that Europe might be freed from Prussian despotism. There must be Justice for the people who now stagger under war debts which exceed thirty thousand million pounds, that Liberty might be saved. There must be Justice for those millions whose homes and lands, ships and property German savagery has spoliated and destroyed. . . .

Not to do justice to all concerned would only leave the world open to fresh calamities. The Treaty is frankly not based upon a general condonation of the events of 1914–1919, it would not be a peace of justice if it were.

As such the Treaty in its present form must be accepted or rejected.

* * *

February 26.

Memorandum of the French Government On the Fixation at the Rhine of the Western Frontier of Germany and on Inter-Allied Occupation of the Rhine Bridges.

I

THE OBJECTS TO BE ATTAINED

The considerations which the French Government submits to the Conference on the subject of the left bank of the Rhine have no selfish character.

They do not tend towards annexations of territories. They aim at the suppression of a common danger and the creation of a common protection.

It is a problem of general interest, a problem which France, the first exposed to the danger it is sought to avert, has the right and duty to place before the Conference, but which directly affects all the Allied and Associated Nations and can be solved only by them conjointly.

The essential aim which the Conference seeks to attain is to prevent by all just means that which has been from ever occurring again.

Now, what happened in 1914 was possible only for one reason: Germany because of her mastery over offensive preparations made by her on the left bank of the river thought herself capable of crushing the democracies, France and Belgium, before the latter could receive the aid of the Overseas Democracies, Great Britain, the Dominions, and the United States.

It was because this was possible that Germany determined to attack.

It is therefore this possibility which must be done away with, by depriving Germany of the means which permitted her to believe in the success of her plan.

In a word there is no question of the aggrandizement of any of the Allied Nations; it is merely a question of placing Germany in a position where she can do no harm by imposing upon her conditions indispensable to the common security of the Western Democracies and of their overseas Allies and associates, as well as to the very existence of France.

There is no question of annexing an inch of German soil; only of depriving Germany of her weapons of offense.

* * *

V

FRENCH INTERESTS IDENTICAL WITH GENERAL INTERESTS

It is now possible to obtain a bird's-eye view of the problem which can be summed up as follows:

(a) In this matter, France claims nothing for herself, neither an inch of territory, nor any right of sovereignty. She does not want to annex the left bank of the Rhine.

What she proposes is the creation in the interest of all of a common protection for all the peaceful democracies, of the League of Nations, of the cause of Liberty and of Peace.

But it is France's duty to add that her bequest, which accords with the general welfare and is free from any selfish design, is of vital necessity to herself and that on its principle she cannot compromise. France sees in it in fact the only immediate and complete guarantee that what she suffered in 1870 and 1914 will not occur again and she owes it to her people, to the dead who must not have died in vain, to the living who wish to rebuild their country in peace and not to stagger beneath overpowering military burdens to obtain this guarantee.

As to the manner of applying this guarantee, the French Government is ready to consult with its Allies with a view to establishing under the most favourable conditions the national, political, and economical system of the regions, access to which it demands shall be forbidden to Germany. To this end, the French Government will accept any suggestions which are not inconsistent with the principle stated.

This principle may be summed up in three paragraphs.

1. No German military force on the left bank of the Rhine, and fixation at the Rhine of the Western frontier of Germany.

2. Occupation of the Rhine bridges by an inter-allied force.

3. No annexation.

This is what under present circumstances France asks as a necessary guarantee of international peace, as the indispensable safeguard of her national existence.

She hopes that all her Allies and Associates will appreciate the *General Interests* of this proposal.

She counts, on the other hand, that they will acknowledge her right and her duty to present and to support this demand for her own sake.

(b) Also this is not the only time that the vital interests of a nation have accorded with the general interests of mankind.

At all times the great naval Powers have asserted — whether the issue were Philip II or Napoleon or William II — that their strength was the only force capable of offsetting imperialistic attempts to control the continent.

It is on this ground that they have justified the maintenance, for their own advantages, of powerful fleets.

Yet, at the same time, they have never concealed the fact that these fleets were a vital necessity to themselves as well.

Of vital necessity to the British Isles and the British Empire — which have made known their refusal to give up any part of that naval power which enabled them to hold the seas against Germany.

Of a vital necessity to the United States, washed by two oceans, requiring safeguards for the export of its natural and industrial resources, and which despite its peaceful policy has for the above reason created a Navy that is even now being further expanded.

For Great Britain, in fact, as well as for the United States, the Navy is a means of pushing away from beyond their coasts the frontier which they would have to defend in case of aggression, and of creating a safety-zone in front of this frontier, in front of their national soil.

For France, the question is the same with this triple difference: that, first, she is not protected from Germany by the seas; that, second, she cannot possibly secure on land the complete guarantee which Great Britain and the United States secured on the sea by the surrender of the German fleet to the Allies, and that finally, the "one to two" ratio between her population and Germany's precludes the hope that in case of war she may ever enjoy the advantage which the naval Powers have always derived from the "two power standards."

For France, as for Great Britain and the United States, it is necessary to create a zone of safety.

This zone the naval Powers create by their fleets, and by the elimination of the German fleet. This zone France, unprotected by the ocean, unable to eliminate the millions of Germans trained to war, must create by the Rhine, by an inter-allied occupation of that river.

If she did not do so, she would once more be exposed, if not to final defeat, at least to a partial destruction of her soil by an enemy invasion.

It is a danger which she never intends to run again.

Moreover, as explained above, the guarantee of peace created by the existence of the naval Powers, could not be of full effect unless the occupation of the Rhine provided a similar guarantee for the Western Democracies.

At a recent meeting of the Supreme Council of the Allies, February 11, 1919, Mr. Winston Churchill and Mr. House showed one after the other what the future has to fear from a Russo-German rapprochement.

In such an event it is not with their fleets that the naval Powers, capable only of establishing a blockade, could defend the continent against an imperialistic aggression.

The naval Powers would still need the possibility of landing on the continent and of fighting there. For that the inter-allied guard of the Rhine is indispensable.

But there is more and one may ask whether, in such case, even the blockade established by the fleets would be effective. Of what use would it be against Germany, mistress of Russia, colonizing and exploiting Russia, if Germany were to strike a successful and decisive blow against France and Belgium, occupying their ports and dominating all the neutral powers of Europe?

This fear was expressed by Mr. House at the meeting of February 15, when he pointed out the danger of an union "of the whole world east of the Rhine." To prevent such an union, or at least to avert its consequences, there is only one way: that the Rhine, henceforth, instead of serving as in the past Germany against the Allies, should protect the Allies against the undertakings of Germany.

In commending this viewpoint to the attention of our Allies and Associates, and more especially of the two great naval Powers, the British Empire and the United States, the French Government is deeply conscious that it is working for peace, just as the naval Powers are conscious that they serve the cause of peace by maintaining or increasing their naval forces.

And just as the naval Powers, in maintaining or increasing their fleets, have no design whatsoever to conquer the seas, so the demand of France as to the guard of the Rhine involves neither gain nor sovereignty nor annexation of territory.

France does not demand for herself the left bank of the Rhine: she would not know what to do with it, and her interest equally with her ideals forbids any such claim.

France demands one thing only. It is that the necessary and only possible and certain measures to prevent the left bank of the Rhine from again becoming a base for German aggression, shall be taken by the Powers now gathered at the Peace Conference.

In other words, with no territorial ambitions, *but deeply imbued with the necessity of creating a protection both national and international,* France looks to an inter-allied occupation of the Rhine for the same results that Great Britain and the United States expect from the maintenance of their naval forces; either more, or less.

In both cases, a national necessity coincides with an international safeguard.

In both cases, even if the second be interpreted in different ways, the first will remain for the country concerned *an obligation subject neither to restriction nor reserve.*

Such is the principle that the French Government begs the Allied and Associated Governments to confirm and sanction by adopting the following decision to be inserted in the provisions of the preliminaries of Peace:

1. *The Western frontier of Germany must be fixed at the Rhine.*

2. *The bridges of the Rhine must be occupied by an inter-allied force.*

3. *The above measures to imply no annexation of territory to the benefit of any Power.*

THE ECONOMIC CONSEQUENCES OF THE PEACE—A BRITISH VIEW

JOHN MAYNARD KEYNES

Just as the term "Keynesian economics" has become commonplace for the student of the modern economy, so the phrase "Economic Consequences of the Peace" has become commonplace for the student of modern diplomatic history. For under that title, John Maynard Keynes published in 1920 one of the most penetrating, controversial and historically influential attacks against the Treaty of Versailles. His book, in fact, created such a stir that it came to affect official policy in Britain as well as significant sectors of public opinion abroad. Principal representative at the Paris Peace Conference of the British Treasury, which he had joined in 1915, Keynes left Paris early in revulsion against the severity of the economic terms of the German treaty. Later to become the leading critic of orthodox economics (through the publication in 1936 of a revolutionary treatise on full employment, inflation, and public investment), after 1919 Keynes remained the leading critic of Versailles.

ABOUT SIX months have now passed by since I published a book entitled "The Economic Consequences of the Peace." In this period the book has been published in the principal languages of the world, and it has been reviewed in many hundreds of journals. The best and the worst have been said of me. But, at any rate, my facts and arguments have been open to the examination of expert critics everywhere; and my conclusions have had to justify themselves before the bar of the educated opinion of the whole world in a manner never required of the half-secret deliberations of Paris.

I am now invited to restate briefly the leading points of my contention and to add a few reflections which the course of events, since I wrote my book, may have suggested. But the space at my disposal is brief, and I must refer to the book itself those readers who are interested in the evidence and arguments in detail.

There are two separate aspects of the peace which we have imposed on the enemy — on the one hand its justice, on the other hand its wisdom and its expediency. I was mainly concerned with the second. But there were certain aspects of the first also with which I thought it my duty to deal carefully.

ITS JUSTICE

The nature of the terms which we were entitled *in justice* to impose depends, in part, on the responsibility of the enemy nations for causing so tremendous a calamity as the late war, and in part on the understanding on which the enemy laid down his arms at the time of the armistice. In my own opinion, it is not possible to lay the entire responsibility for the state of affairs out of which the war arose on any single nation; it was engendered, in part at least, by the essential character of international politics and rivalries during the latter part of the nineteenth century, by militarism everywhere (certainly in Russia as well as

From John Maynard Keynes, "The Peace of Versailles," *Everybody's Magazine*, XLIII (September, 1920), pp. 36–41.

in Germany and Austria-Hungary), and by the universally practiced policies of economic imperialism; it had its seeds deep in the late history of Europe.

But I believe, nevertheless, that Germany bears a special and peculiar responsibility for the war itself, for its universal and devastating character, and for its final development into a combat without quarter for mastery or defeat. A criminal may be the outcome of his environment, but he is none the less a criminal.

The evidence which has become public in the past year has convinced me that, during the weeks preceding August, 1914, persons in power in Germany deliberately provoked the war and intended that it should commence when it did. If this be so, the accepted standards of international justice entitled us to impose, at Germany's expense, any terms which might be calculated to make good some part of the destruction done, to heal Europe's wounds, to preserve and perpetuate peace, and to terrify future malefactors.

Even so, however, it was our duty to look more to the future than to the past, to distinguish between the late rulers of Germany on the one hand and her common people and unborn posterity on the other, and to be sure that our acts were guided by magnanimity and wisdom more than by revenge or hatred. It was also proper for us to feel and practice some measure of humility at the conclusion of so terrible and extraordinary a struggle, and not to elevate ourselves and our Allies, in boastful and unseemly language, to a level of morality and of international disinterestedness which, whatever the faults of others, we can not claim. But above all, should not the future peace of the world have been our highest and guiding motive? Men of all nations had suffered together, the victims of a curse deep-seated in the past history and present weakness of the European race. The lifting of the curse was a better object in the treaty, if universal justice were our aim, than its relentless execution.

ITS HONORABLENESS

But there was another aspect of justice, more earthly than the high topics which have just occupied us — the question of our promises, in reliance on which the enemy had capitulated. Beginning with the invasion of Belgium, the Allied countries had pronounced the sacredness of engagements and the maintenance of international good faith as among their principal objects. Only thus, in the judgment of the considered wisdom of the world, only by the establishment of the rule of law as between nations, can national egotisms be tempered and the stability of settlements be preserved. It was therefore peculiarly incumbent upon us to practice what we had preached, and even to be so scrupulous as not to take advantage of an ambiguous phrase.

To understand the peace, therefore, and its effect on general confidence in the fairness of the Allies, we have to remember the history of the negotiations which began with the German note of October 5, 1918, and concluded with President Wilson's note of November 5, 1918. . . .

* * *

THE ARMISTICE CONTRACT

The nature of the contract between Germany and the Allies resulting from this exchange of documents is plain and unequivocal. The terms of the peace are to be in accordance with the addresses of the President, and the purpose of the Peace Conference is "to discuss the details of their application." The circumstances of the contract were of an unusually solemn and binding character; for one of the conditions of it was that Germany should agree to armistice terms which were to be such as would leave her helpless.

What, then, was the substance of this contract to which the Allies had bound themselves? I have examined this in detail in my book. In a word, we were committed to a peace based upon the Fourteen Points and upon the principle that "there shall be no annexations, no contributions, no punitive damages."

It is still maintained by some persons that the enemy surrendered unconditionally and that we are in no way bound by the engagements outlined above. This has been maintained lately, for example, in a lengthy article contributed to the New York *Times* by General Greene. Other advocates of the treaty stand upon the other leg and maintain that, while we are bound by the Fourteen Points, the peace treaty is in substantial conformity with them. This, I understand, is the attitude of President Wilson. I am reckoned a hostile critic of the President because I believe that he holds this attitude sincerely, having been partly deceived and partly self-deceived, his thought and feeling being here cast in what, for lack of a more descriptive phrase, I termed a theological mold. His friends argue, however, that he was well aware of what he was doing in Paris and deliberately sacrificed some part of his professions in the interests of the higher political expediency.

THE ENIGMA OF WILSON

The extraordinary story of hopes, ideals, weaknesses, failures and disappointments, of which the President has been the leading figure and eponymous hero, will interest and perplex mankind as long as history is read and the hearts of the great ones are the subject of the curious exploration of the multitude. Was Hamlet mad or feigning? Was the President sick or cunning? On what a stage he played, and with what forfeits! Ruling the destinies of nations, now with the words of the philosopher and next with the realities of power; with the voices of heaven at one ear and the party managers at the other; proud and timorous; lofty and small; disinterested and ambitious; soaring to the rarest heights of terrestrial fortune, and there smitten by the blindness of Apollo and the plagues of Egypt.

If the President loves fame, let him be satisfied. Posterity remembers the mixed characters of history who have a star and it fails them. The Emperor William exhibits for us the fluctuations of fate. But he belongs to the satyric drama, a victim of the buffoonery of the gods, whose story may instruct but will not perplex us. For the President a grander niche is waiting, where he and his story will symbolize and illustrate some of the mingled and mysterious strains in our common nature.

Yet I, at any rate, though I have tried to express what I saw, and am not shaken in my opinions by the subsequent passage of events, would shrink from controversy with critics on so doubtful and perplexed an issue as the feelings and the motives of an individual. I have put on record in my analysis of the President the impression produced on a single observer, and I claim no more for it. I wrote in a moment of disappointment, but, to the best of my ability, in a spirit of greater historical objectivity than some of my critics have given me credit for. Events themselves have surely shown that he was not wise, and even that he was deluded. But I do not forget that he, alone among the statesmen of Paris, sought ideal aims, and sincerely pursued throughout the Conference the future peace of the world as his supreme and governing purpose. Even in the futile stubbornness of the past few months an element of nobility has been present. . . .

But there remains the question — greater than that of the actions and motives of individuals — whether in fact we have kept faith with our enemies. I have maintained that on certain matters we have not kept faith, the most important instance within the economic sphere, which was my particular subject-matter, being the inclusion in our reparation claims of huge sums for military pensions and separation allowances, which greatly swell the bill and to which we are not entitled. Our treatment of the Saar Valley, of tariffs, and of Germany's river system afford other examples.

Let me here limit myself to the reparation claims. I venture to assert that my criticism of these claims has not been seriously controverted by any one. It has been stated, since my book appeared, that the President's own advisers in Paris informed him that these claims were illegitimate. Many critics have passed over in silence this particular issue. Yet if it is in fact the case that we have not kept our engagements, is it not a matter of some importance to the national honor of each one of the allied and associated countries, and to the moral government of the world?

Those who have defended the treaty on this issue have done so on the most extraordinary grounds. I select below some of the commoner lines of argument. Some say that Germany, if she had won, would not have kept faith with us, and that this fact absolves us from being overscrupulous with her; the enemy, being themselves unjust — this argument asserts — are not entitled to better treatment in return.

Others say that the information we now have makes it probable that Germany could have been compelled to surrender unconditionally, and that for this reason the President's *pourparlers* before the armistice lose much of their binding character.

Others point out that our engagements were in part vaguely expressed; that they were not cast in legal form; that there is no one to enforce them; and that they can not therefore constitute a "contract." (Imagine, however, with what indignation these same apologists would explode before a similar argument on the lips of a German.)

Others, again, discover that the President was exceeding his powers in his preliminary negotiations as to the basis of the peace, in reliance on which the enemy laid down his arms; and that his promises consequently bound no one.

These are all of them types of man's eternal reasons for not keeping his promises, and their roots are in human nature. But they ill accord with the victorious issue of a crusade for the sanctity of international agreements.

THE TREATY'S WISDOM

With these brief comments I pass from the justice of the treaty, which can not be ignored even when it is not our central topic, to its wisdom and its expediency. Under these heads my criticism of the treaty is double. In the first place, this treaty ignores the economic solidarity of Europe, and by aiming at the destruction of the economic life of Germany it threatens the health and prosperity of the Allies themselves. In the second place, by making demands the execution of which is in the literal sense impossible, it stultifies itself and leaves Europe more unsettled than it found it. The treaty, by overstepping the limits of the possible, has in practice settled nothing. The true settlement still remains to be made out of the ashes of the present and the disillusionment of the future, when the imposture of Paris is recognized for what it is.

For reasons of historical experience, which are easily understood, and with which all men must sympathize (however profoundly we believe that France will deal to herself as well as to her enemy a fatal wound if she yields to them), there were powerful influences in Paris demanding for the future security of France that the peace should complete the destruction of the economic life of Central Europe, which the war had gone far to consummate.

THE SHATTERED HEART OF EUROPE

The German economic system as it existed before the war depended on three main factors:

1. Overseas commerce, as represented by her mercantile marine, her colonies, her foreign investments, her exports, and the overseas connections of her merchants.

2. The exploitation of her coal and iron and the industries built upon them.

3. Her transport and tariff system.

Of these the first, while not the least important, was certainly the most vulnerable. The treaty aims at the systematic destruction of all three, but principally the first two.

Germany has ceded to the Allies all the vessels of her mercantile marine exceeding sixteen hundred tons gross, half the vessels between one thousand tons and sixteen hundred tons, and one-quarter of her trawlers and other fishing boats. The cession is comprehensive, including not only vessels flying the German flag, but also all vessels owned by Germans but flying other flags, and all vessels under construction as well as those afloat. Further, Germany undertakes, if required, to build for the Allies such types of ships as they may specify, up to two hundred thousand tons annually for five years, the value of these ships being credited to Germany against what is due from her for reparation. Thus the German mercantile marine is swept from the seas and can not be restored for many years to come on a scale adequate to meet the requirements of her own commerce.

Germany has ceded to the Allies "all her rights and titles over her overseas possessions." This cession not only applies to sovereignty but extends on unfavorable terms to government property, all of which, including railways, must be surrendered without payment. Further, in distinction from the practice ruling in the case of most similar cessions in recent history, the property and persons of private German nationals, as distinct from their Government, are also injuriously affected. Not only are German sovereignty and German influence extirpated from the whole of her former overseas possessions, but the persons and property of her nationals resident or owning property in those parts are deprived of legal status and legal security.

The provisions just outlined in regard to the private property of Germans in the ex-German colonies apply equally to private German property in Alsace-Lorraine, except in so far as the French Government may choose to grant exceptions.

The expropriation of German private property is not limited, however, to the ex-German colonies and Alsace-Lorraine. The cumulative effect of a series of complicated provisions, which I have examined in detail in my book, is to deprive Germany (or rather to empower the Allies so to deprive her at their will — it is not yet accomplished) of everything she possesses outside her own frontiers as laid down in the treaty. Not only are her overseas investments taken and her connections destroyed, but the same

process of extirpation is applied in the territories of her former allies and of her immediate neighbors by land.

The above provisions relate to Germany's external wealth. Those relating to coal and iron are more important in respect of their ultimate consequences to Germany's internal industrial economy than for the money value immediately involved. The German Empire has been built more truly on coal and iron than on blood and iron. The skilled exploitation of the great coalfields of the Ruhr, Upper Silesia and the Saar alone made possible the development of the steel, chemical, and electrical industries which established her as the first industrial nation of continental Europe. One-third of Germany's population lives in towns of more than twenty thousand inhabitants, an industrial concentration which is only possible on a foundation of coal and iron. In striking, therefore, at her coal supply, those who sought her economic destruction were not mistaking their target.

COAL

The coal clauses of the treaty are, however, among those which are likely, by reason of the technical impossibility of their execution, to defeat their own object. If the plebiscite results in Germany's losing the coal districts of Upper Silesia, the treaty will have deprived her of territory from which not far short of one-third of her total coal supply was previously derived. Out of the coal that remains to her Germany is required, quite rightly, to make good for ten years the estimated loss which France has incurred by the destruction and damage of war in the coalfields of her northern provinces, such deliveries not to exceed twenty million tons in each of the first five years or eight million tons annually thereafter. She has also, over and above this, for ten years to deliver annually seven million tons to France, eight million tons to Belgium, and from four million five hundred thousand tons to eight million five hundred thousand tons to Italy.

I have estimated that this would leave

Germany with about sixty million tons annually against domestic requirements, which, on the prewar basis of industry in her remaining territory, would amount to one hundred and ten million tons. In short, Germany could only execute the coal demands of the treaty by abandoning the bulk of her industries and returning to the status of an agricultural country. In this case many millions of her present population could obtain neither work nor food (nor, indeed, facilities of emigration). Yet it is not to be supposed that the population of any country will submit year after year to an export which dooms many of them to starvation and even to death. The thing is humanly and politically impossible. Men will not die so obediently to the dictates of a document. The coal clauses of the treaty are not being executed and never will be.

But in this event the treaty settles nothing, and the extent of the coal deliveries remains as a source of perpetual friction, uncertainty and inefficiency, which will inhibit the industrial activity of all the European countries alike which are parties to it. The coal will not be delivered; it may not even be mined. No plans which look ahead can be made by anyone. The commodity will be the subject of a perpetual scramble; and even of military occupations and of bloodshed. For, as the result of many various causes, the coal position of all Europe is nearly desperate, and no country will lightly surrender its treaty rights. I affirm, therefore, that the coal clauses are inexpedient and disastrous, and full of danger not only for the economic efficiency but for the political peace of the European continent.

IRON

The provisions relating to iron ore require less detailed attention, though their effects are destructive. They require less attention, because they are in large measure inevitable. Almost exactly seventy-five per cent of the iron ore raised in Germany in 1913 came from Alsace-Lorraine. But while Lorraine contained seventy-five per cent of Germany's iron ore, only twenty-five per cent of her blast-furnaces and of her foundries lay within Lorraine and the Saar basin together, a large proportion of the ore being carried into Germany proper. Thus here, as elsewhere, political considerations cut disastrously across economic.

In a régime of free trade and free economic intercourse it would be of little consequence that iron lay on one side of a political frontier and labor, coal and blast-furnaces on the other. But it seems certain, calculating on the present passions and impulses of European capitalistic society, that the effective iron output of Europe will be diminished by a new political frontier (which sentiment and historic justice require), because nationalism and private interest are thus allowed to impose a new economic frontier along the same lines. These latter considerations are allowed, in the present governance of Europe, to prevail over the intense need of the continent for the most sustained and efficient production to repair the destruction of war and to satisfy the insistence of labor for a larger reward.

Thus in its coal and iron clauses the treaty strikes at organization, and by the destruction of organization impairs yet further the reduced wealth of the whole community.

There remain those treaty provisions which relate to the transport and the tariff systems of Germany. These parts of the treaty have not nearly the importance and significance of those discussed hitherto. They are pin-pricks, interferences and vexations, not so much objectionable for their solid consequences as dishonorable to the Allies in the light of their professions. I can not spare space in this brief article to consider them in the detail they deserve. Taken in their entirety, the economic clauses of the treaty are comprehensive, and little has been overlooked which might impoverish Germany now or obstruct her development in future. So situated, Germany is to make payments of money, on a scale and in a manner about to be examined.

The treaty's claims for an indemnity may

be divided into two parts: those which, in accordance with our pre-armistice engagements, we were entitled to make if we judged it expedient to do so, and those which, in my judgment, we had no right to make. The first category includes as its chief items all the direct damages to civilian life and property for which Germany was responsible, more particularly in the invaded and occupied areas of France, Belgium, and Serbia, by air-raids, and by warfare of submarines. It includes also compensation for the improper treatment of interned civilians and for the loot of food, raw materials, live stock, machinery, household effects, timber, and the like; and the repayment of fines and requisitions levied on the towns of France and Belgium. I have ventured as a very rough estimate to calculate the total of these items at the following figures:

Belgium	$2,500,000,000
France	4,000,000,000
Great Britain	2,850,000,000
Other Allies	1,250,000,000
	$10,600,000,000

I need not impress on the reader that there is much guesswork in the above, and the figure for France in particular has been criticized on the ground that it is too low. But I feel some confidence that the general magnitude, as distinct from the precise figures, is not very erroneous; and this may be expressed by the statement that a claim against Germany, based on the interpretation of the pre-armistice engagements of the Allied Powers which is adopted above, would assuredly be found to exceed eight billion and to fall short of fifteen billion.

INDEMNITY DEMANDS

This is the amount of the claim which we were entitled to present to the enemy. I believe that it would have been a wise and just act to have asked the German Government at the peace negotiations to agree to a sum of ten billion in final settlement, without further examination of particulars. This would have provided an immediate and certain solution, and would have required

from Germany a sum which, if she were granted certain indulgences, it might not have proved entirely impossible for her to pay. This sum should have been divided up among the Allies themselves on a basis of need and general equity.

But the question was not settled on its merits, and the above figure is far from representing the whole of our actual claims under the treaty. As a compromise between keeping the letter of our engagements and demanding the entire cost of the war, which French and British politicians had promised to their constituents from the platform, Paris decided to include a claim, which seemed plausible in itself, which recommended itself to sentiment, and which amounted to a large sum; and Germany has been required to discharge in their entirety all military pensions and separation allowances paid or to be paid, which have arisen out of the war. I have estimated that this adds to the bill an aggregate sum of twenty-five billion dollars made up as follows:

France	$12,000,000,000
British Empire	7,000,000,000
Italy	2,500,000,000
Others (including the U.S.)	3,500,000,000
	$25,000,000,000

Adding this figure to my maximum estimate of fifteen billion dollars, we have a total claim against Germany of about forty billion dollars. While the details making up this total have been criticized and much higher figures have been mentioned (as, for example, seventy-five billion dollars by M. Klotz, then finance minister of France), the world has, generally speaking, accepted my figure as representing the facts as nearly as is at present possible, and as supplying a reasonable basis of discussion.

THE BLANK CHECK

The reader will observe that this figure is mine, and that no final amount is specified by the treaty itself, which fixes no definite sum as representing Germany's liability. This feature has been the subject of very general criticism, that it is equally inconvenient to Germany and to the Allies themselves that she should not know what she has to pay or they what they are to receive. The method, apparently contemplated by the treaty, of arriving at the final result over a period of many months by an addition of hundreds of thousands of individual claims for damage to land, farm buildings and chickens, is evidently impracticable, and the reasonable course would have been for both parties to compound for a round sum without examination of details. If this round sum had been named in the treaty, the settlement would have been placed on a more businesslike basis.

But this was impossible for two reasons. Two different kinds of false statements had been widely promulgated, one as to Germany's capacity to pay, the other as to the amount of the Allies' just claims in respect of the devastated areas. The fixing of either of these figures presented a dilemma. A figure for Germany's prospective capacity to pay, not too much in excess of the estimates of most candid and well-informed authorities, would have fallen hopelessly far short of popular expectations both in England and in France. On the other hand, a definite figure for damage done which would not disastrously disappoint the expectations that had been raised in France and Belgium might have been incapable of substantiation under challenge.

By far the safest course for the politicians was, therefore, to mention no figure at all; and from this necessity a great deal of the complication of the reparation scheme essentially springs.

According to the letter of the treaty, any part of the sum eventually determined as due which remains unpaid from time to time is to accumulate at interest at five per cent, while the earlier installments of payment are contemplated as follows: Up to May 1, 1921, Germany is to make lump-sum payments, in cash, kind and bearer bonds, so as to bring the net sum available for reparation to fifteen billion dollars. These bearer bonds carry interest at two and one-half per cent per annum from 1921

to 1925, and at five per cent plus one per cent for amortization thereafter. Assuming, therefore, that Germany is not able to provide any appreciable surplus toward reparation before 1921, she will have to find a sum of three hundred and seventy-five million dollars annually from 1921 to 1925, and nine hundred million dollars annually thereafter.

As soon as the Reparation Commission is satisfied that Germany can do better than this, five per cent bearer bonds are to be issued for a further ten billion dollars, the rate of amortization being determined by the commission hereafter. This would bring the annual payment to one billion four hundred million dollars without allowing anything for the discharge of the capital of the last ten billion dollars.

Germany's liability, however, is not limited to twenty-five billion dollars, and the Reparation Commission is to demand further instalments of bearer bonds until the total enemy liability has been provided for. On the basis of my estimate of forty billion dollars for the total liability, this balance will be fifteen billion dollars. Assuming interest at five per cent, this will raise the annual payment to two billion one hundred and fifty million dollars without allowance for amortization.

But even this is not all. There is a further provision of devastating significance. Bonds representing payments in excess of fifteen billion dollars are not to be issued until the commission is satisfied that Germany can meet the interest on them. But this does not mean that interest is remitted in the meantime. As from May 1, 1921, the capital sum of indebtedness is rolling up all the time at compound interest. The effect of this provision toward increasing the burden is enormous, on the assumption that Germany can not pay very large sums at first.

At five percent compound interest a capital sum doubles itself in fifteen years. On the assumption that Germany can not pay more than seven hundred and fifty million dollars annually until 1936 (i.e. five per cent interest on fifteen billion dollars) the twenty-five billion dollars on which interest is deferred will have risen to fifty billion dollars, carrying an annual interest charge of two billion five hundred million dollars.

AN AVALANCHE OF DEBT

That is to say, even if Germany pays seven hundred and fifty million dollars annually up to 1936, she will nevertheless owe us at that date more than half as much again as she now does (sixty-five billion dollars as compared with forty billion dollars). From 1936 onward she will have to pay to us three billion two hundred and fifty million dollars annually in order to keep pace with the interest alone. At the end of any year in which she pays less than this sum she will owe more than she did at the beginning of it. And if she is to discharge the capital sum in thirty years from 1936, i.e., in forty-eight years from the armistice, she must pay an additional six hundred and fifty million dollars annually, making three billion nine hundred million dollars in all.

It is, in my judgment, as certain as anything can be, for reasons which I will summarize in a moment, that Germany can not pay anything approaching this sum. Until the treaty is altered, therefore, Germany has in effect engaged herself to hand over to the Allies the whole of her surplus production in perpetuity.

This is not less the case because the Reparation Commission has been given discretionary powers to vary the rate of interest, and to postpone and even to cancel the capital indebtedness. In the first place, some of these powers can only be exercised if the commission or the governments represented on it are *unanimous*. But also, which is perhaps more important, it will be the *duty* of the Reparation Commission, until there has been a unanimous and far-reaching change of the policy which the treaty represents, to extract from Germany year after year the maximum sum obtainable. There is a great difference between fixing a definite sum, which, though large, is within Germany's capacity to pay and yet to retain a little for herself, and fixing a sum far beyond her capacity, which is then to be reduced at the discretion of a foreign commission, acting with the object of obtaining each year the maximum which the circumstances of that year permit. For the first still leaves her with some slight incentive for enterprise, energy, and hope.

GERMANY'S CAPACITY TO PAY

How is Germany placed, in the situation in which the rest of the treaty leaves her, for discharging a vast obligation?

It is evident that Germany's pre-war capacity to pay an annual foreign tribute has not been unaffected by the almost total loss of her colonies, her overseas connections, her mercantile marine, and her foreign properties; by the cession of ten percent of her territory and population, of one-third of her coal and of three-quarters of her iron ore; by two million casualties among men in the prime of life; by the starvation of her people for four years; by the burden of a vast war debt; by the depreciation of her currency to less than one-seventh its former value; by the disruption of her allies and their territories; by revolution at home and Bolshevism on her borders; and by all the unmeasured ruin in strength and hope of four years of all-swallowing war and final defeat.

All this, one would have supposed, is evident. Yet most estimates of a great indemnity from Germany depend on the assumption that she is in a position to conduct in the future a vastly greater trade than ever she has had in the past.

The forms in which Germany can discharge her debt are three and three only: (1) immediately transferable wealth in the form of gold, ships, and foreign securities; (2) the value of property in ceded territory or surrendered under the armistice; and (3) annual payments spread over a term of years, partly in cash and partly in materials such as coal products, potash, and dyes. There is no other way whatever.

In my book I have analyzed in detail the value of the items under the first two heads.

What has occurred since I made my estimate has tended to the conclusion that this estimate is too high rather than too low; nor have my figures been seriously challenged by any one. The general conclusion of this examination of the available data is that a sum of from five hundred million dollars to one billion dollars is the utmost that can be available after payment of the costs of the armies of occupation.

It will perhaps assist the reader to visualize how trifling the tangible and transferable wealth of Germany is, in relation to the fantastic magnitudes mentioned above, if I select one important special item. The total value of the German mercantile marine, which under the treaty the Allies are to obtain for themselves, is probably overstated at six hundred million dollars — six hundred million dollars toward a total liability of forty billion dollars. The vast expenditures of the war, the inflation of prices, and the depreciation of currency, leading up to a complete instability of the unit of value, joined to the fact that what we believed to be the limits of possibility have been so enormously exceeded and those who founded their expectations on the past have been so often wrong, have made the man in the street lose all sense of number and magnitude in matters of finance. But we must endeavor to regain our sense of proportion.

If the amount of Germany's immediately transferable property is unimportant, it follows that the Reparation Commission must mainly depend on future annual payments. There is literally only one way in which such payments can be made (apart from temporary loans to Germany by foreign countries), namely, by the exports of Germany exceeding her imports. It follows, therefore, that a rational estimate of the possibilities of the case can only be made on the basis of the examination of the trade figures of Germany before the war and of the possible expansion of the export items.

It is not possible within the limits of the space here at my disposal to enter into the details of this examination. But my broad conclusion is that in the actual facts of the case there is no reasonable probability of Germany's being able to make payments in excess of five hundred million dollars annually. This figure has not been challenged in detail by any one, and has been supported, as being in the neighborhood of the best estimate, by many distinguished authorities.

HER EXPORT POWERS

A few leading facts may be summarized. The staple exports of Germany are: (1) Iron and steel goods; (2) machinery; (3) coal, coke and briquettes; (4) woolen goods; (5) cotton goods; these five classes between them accounting before the war for nearly forty percent of the total exports. As regards two of the categories, namely, cotton and woolen goods, the increase of an export trade is dependent upon an increase of the import of the raw material, since Germany produces no cotton and practically no wool. These trades are therefore incapable of great expansion unless Germany is given facilities for securing these raw materials (which can only be at the expense of the Allies) in excess of the pre-war standard of consumption, and even then the effective increase is not the gross value of the exports, but only the difference between the value of the manufactured exports and of the imported raw material.

As regards the other three categories — namely, machinery, iron goods, and coal — Germany's capacity to increase her exports will have been taken from her by the cessions of territory in Poland, Upper Silesia, and Alsace-Lorraine. As has been pointed out already, these districts accounted for nearly one-third of Germany's production of coal. But they also supplied no less than three-quarters of her iron-ore production and thirty-eight percent of her blast-furnaces. Unless, therefore, Alsace-Lorraine and Upper Silesia send their iron ore to Germany proper, to be worked up — which will involve an increase in the imports for which she will have to find payment — so far from any increase in export trade being possible, a decrease is inevitable.

Yet an enormously increased export is necessary. For, so far from Germany's exports exceeding her imports before the war, her imports exceeded her exports on the average of the five years ending 1913 by about three hundred and seventy million dollars. On the assumptions, therefore, (1) that we do not specially favor Germany over ourselves in supplies of such raw materials as cotton and wool (the world's supply of which is limited); (2) that France, having secured the iron-ore deposits, makes a serious attempt to secure the blast-furnaces and the steel trade also; (3) that Germany is not encouraged and assisted to undercut the iron and other trades of the Allies in overseas markets; and (4) that a substantial preference is not given to German goods in the British Empire and other Allied countries, it becomes evident by examination of the specific items that not much is practicable.

I reach, therefore, the final conclusion that, including all methods of payment — immediately transferable wealth, ceded property, and an annual tribute — ten billion dollars is a safe maximum figure of Germany's capacity to pay. In all the actual circumstances, I do not believe that she can pay as much.

A capacity of forty billion dollars or even of twenty-five billion dollars is, therefore, not within the limits of reasonable possibility. It is for those who believe that Germany can make an annual payment amounting to thousands of millions of dollars to say *in what specific commodities* they intend this payment to be made, and *in what markets* the goods are to be sold. Until they proceed to some degree of detail, and are able to produce some tangible argument in favor of their conclusions, they do not deserve to be believed.

A DEAD TREATY

Such, in brief, are the economic provisions of the Treaty of Versailles, which the United States has refused to ratify and most of Europe would now unwrite if it could. A year has passed since it came into existence, and authority has already passed from it — not, in my judgment, because there has been much softening of sentiment toward Germany, but because the treaty is no treaty, because it is now generally recognized that in truth it settles nothing. After what has passed, Europe requires above all a *settlement,* and this the treaty has not given it. If you pledge a man to perform the impossible, you are no nearer a decision as to what in fact he is to do; for his pledge is, necessarily, a dead letter. The reparation and coal clauses of the treaty are its most important economic features. But being composed of foolish, idle words, having no relation to the real facts, they are without practical effect, and they leave the prospects of the future undetermined.

What, then, are we to do? Before I venture an answer, there is one element in the attitude of the United States to the treaty which deserves attention. The United States has refused to ratify the treaty; the United States gets nothing out of the treaty; the ideals of the vast majority of the inhabitants of the United States are probably at variance with the treaty; even at Paris it was the representatives of the United States who fought most sincerely and resolutely for the modification of the treaty — yet it is in the United States that the treaty now finds its most whole-hearted defenders.

THE SITUATION HERE

The explanation of the paradox is to be found, I think, in this: in England the treaty was swallowed in the first instance without much criticism or comment; it has never become in any intense degree a party question; Mr. Lloyd George himself now appears among those most willing to modify it; and consequently there is no vested interest in defending it. But in the United States the treaty has become a bitter party question. The President, in a spirit, as I believe, of sincere delusion, or, as his friends maintain, of calculated wisdom, has maneuvered himself or been maneuvered into the position of defending the integral acceptance of the document. The personal adherents of the President must follow his single track. An American professor or an American lawyer back from the Conference writes about the treaty in newspapers articles of hot eulogy, such as are not common in Europe. My own American colleagues from Paris, whose views I so much shared and whose labors against the treaty I so much admired, now, alas! find themselves committed by loyalty to an honored chief to representing the treaty, what no one in Europe now thinks it, as an instrument of substantial wisdom. Truly the President carries his own cross, doomed by a perverse fate to support a settlement which has at the same time shattered his prestige and defeated his ideals.

It will therefore be difficult, I fear — though I speak at a distance and without knowledge — so long as the treaty remains a party issue, for the United States to approach its great problems in the impartial and disinterested spirit which their special position makes possible and will, I believe, eventually make actual.

REMEDIES

From this necessary digression I return to the question of the policy of the immediate future. For my own part I hold with increasing conviction that the revision of the treaty is the necessary and inevitable first step forward. In the book which I wrote nearly a year ago I proposed various other remedies, including an international loan and the cancellation of war debt between Allies. I believe that these, perhaps utopian, plans were of value a year ago; they may be of value again a year or two hence, though by that time the circumstances of the day may demand a different solution in detail if not in spirit. But I concede that at this moment of time the attitude of the United States and the actual condition of Europe have combined to render them impracticable. Until by the revision of the treaty we are furnished with a sound foundation on which to build, the best laid schemes will fail.

Let me add that I differ profoundly from those who, admitting the imperfections of the treaty, look for succor to the provisions contained in it for its progressive modification in practice by the unanimous consent of the leading Allies. The difference between revising the treaty at once and progressively modifying it under the force of circumstances is the difference between building a firm foundation and underpinning day by day a tottering structure.

THE FUTURE

This revision is bound, as matters now are, to be primarily the affair of Europe. But it will be a disaster for the world if America isolates herself. I do not regret that the Congress of the United States has repudiated the treaty of Paris. But I pray that out of the ashes of this treaty and out of the embryonic shapes of the present League of Nations a new settlement and a new League may even now arise which will command the allegiance of all men.

The current of time seems to move slowly sometimes to the passengers upon its surface. In the interval, perhaps a short one, which must now elapse, I hope that we, the various peoples of the world, may abstain from vulgar and unmerciful words. It has been said that individuals everywhere are lovable and all nations detestable. There are very few nations at this time against which an accuser could not draw a just and injurious indictment. But Burke spoke deeply when he declared that he did not know the method of drawing up an indictment against a whole people. "I really think," he added, "that for wise men this is not judicious, for sober men not decent, for minds tinctured with humanity not mild and merciful."

THE ECONOMIC CONSEQUENCES OF
MR. KEYNES—A FRENCH VIEW

ETIENNE MANTOUX

Keynes' massive attack against the economic terms of Versailles did not go unchallenged. In all Allied states, and particularly in France, there was strong and widespread feeling that the Germans should, and indeed could, be made to discharge all economic obligations imposed by the peace treaty and subsequent inter-Allied agreements. The most noteworthy statement of this position and one intended directly as a reply to Keynes, came from the pen of a brilliant young French economist, Etienne Mantoux. Son of the official interpreter in 1919 to the innermost councils of the peace conference, young Mantoux completed the famous work from which the following passages are reprinted, just as World War II was approaching its climax. Then, ten days before the curtain fell on the great military drama of his own generation, Etienne Mantoux died on the advanced front line in Germany.

M R. KEYNES had assailed the statesmen of the Conference for their failure to apprehend "that the most serious of the problems which claimed their attention were not political or territorial but financial and economic, and that the perils of the future lay not in frontiers or sovereignties but in food, coal, and transport." Compared to these, other issues, such as territorial adjustment and the balance of power, were unreal or "insignificant." How often do we hear this pronouncement quoted today as the unheeded lesson that must this time become our inspiration! But in view of the wealth of prophecies and warnings that were issued at the time, the merit has not yet perhaps been quite fairly apportioned among them all. As for his own, Mr. Keynes did not appear to believe that they had much to do with the unfurling of policies and events. "The *Prophecy*," he wrote some years afterwards, in the preface to a volume where he had collected some of his miscellaneous writings, "has been more successful than the *Persuasion*."

The Economic Consequences of the Peace was read all over the world. By 1924 the book had been translated into eleven languages, and its various editions had run into some 140,000 copies. Perhaps only Edmund Burke's *Reflections on the Revolution in France* may be said to have wielded over the destinies of Europe such a widespread and immediate influence.

Its success, to be sure, was far from uniform. Naturally enough, enthusiasm was loudest in Germany (even though nothing in the book could be sensibly called "pro-German"). And although Mr. Keynes had written most explicitly: "France, in my judgment, in spite of her policy at the Peace Conference, a policy largely traceable to her sufferings, has the greatest claims on our generosity," it was received in France with a stupefied indignation. In Great Britain and the United States, reactions were

From Etienne Mantoux, *The Carthaginian Peace or The Economic Consequences of Mr. Keynes* (New York, 1952), pp. 6–11, 32–43, 46–49, 155–159, 187–188. Reprinted by permission.

mixed: "Comfort for Germany," wrote the London *Times*. Several of the American delegates to the Conference — Messrs. D. H. Miller, J. F. Dulles, Clive Day — protested sharply against what they called the book's misrepresentations, and challenged its general conclusions. Most of the hostile reviewers reprimanded the author for his lack of "political sense." Some said the book was academic, others that it was reckless. But very few attempted to criticize in any detail Mr. Keynes's findings on the economic side of the Peace Treaty; and such opponents as dared to affront his indefatigable pugnacity were soon overwhelmed by the mounting tide of public opinion. "*The Nation, Westminster Gazette, Sunday Chronicle, Athenaeum, Fortnightly Review*, all recognized at once the authentic and masterly, and freely welcomed it," wrote Lord Stamp several years later. "The general instructed chorus in America was with Keynes. . . ." And only two months after the publication of his book, Mr. Keynes was writing to *The Times*: "I have been criticized on various grounds, personal and otherwise. But no one has made a serious attempt to traverse my main conclusions. The illuminating influence of time has done its work, and these conclusions no longer conflict with the instructed opinion of the day."

Thus, however Prophecy might fare, Persuasion, at any rate, had so far been successful; its effects were soon to be manifest.

For good or ill, the whole structure of the Treaty of Versailles had to rest upon the active and continuous support of all those who had designed it. Among them, America was foremost. Had America been absent from the War, the end might have been very different; so might have been the Treaty in the absence of America at the Conference. And without her participation in future, much of the Treaty was meaningless: for certain concrete guarantees had been abandoned in exchange for America's promise to give her own guarantee to the peace settlement. "The whole Treaty,"

wrote Mr. Harold Nicolson, "had been deliberately, and ingeniously, framed by Mr. Wilson himself to render American co-operation essential." Should this co-operation fail to materialize, the whole equipoise of Europe, so precarious already, might once again collapse.

Contemptuous as he was then of the balance of power and other such issues, Mr. Keynes probably did not attach much importance to this aspect of the problem. But no one could have been better convinced than he was of the need for America's participation in the economic reconstruction of Europe; for his positive programme of remedies implied, as an indispensable condition, not only a cancellation of inter-Allied indebtedness with the main burden falling upon the United States, but a new loan the major part of which was to come out of American pockets. Just as the execution of the Treaty was dependent upon American co-operation, so was the policy advocated in its stead dependent upon American goodwill. It seemed essential that America should not be persuaded to let Europe stew in its own juice.

Now even before the Treaty had been signed, the future attitude of the United States was arousing the gravest misgivings. News from across the Atlantic revealed increasing criticism of the President's person and policies. Many were beginning to wonder whether the public was still behind him, and whether in the end the Treaty would be ratified. Theodore Roosevelt had warned Europe that the President no longer commanded the confidence of the nation. In Congress, opposition was becoming louder every day. "As it dawned gradually upon them (as upon us)," Mr. Harold Nicolson has said of his relations with the American delegates, "that America was asking Europe to make vital sacrifices for an ideal which America herself would be the first to betray, a helpless embarrassment descended upon both of us. The ghastly suspicion that the American people would not honour the signature of their own delegates was never mentioned between us; it became the ghost at all our feasts." The months that followed the return of the President to America gave increasing confirmation of these suspicions; and in the summer and fall of 1919, while Keynes's book was being written, the President was locked in mortal struggle to secure the adoption of the Treaty against the rising tide of opposition.

Now no one can say with any certainty what course history would have taken if America's political co-operation with Europe had continued after 1919. But at the time it was not unwarranted to assume — particularly on the part of any one bent, as was Mr. Keynes, on the softening of the Treaty's provisions — that in view of the attitude taken over certain questions by the American delegates at Paris, the best chance of having the Treaty modified in the sense desired was first to secure the continuance of America's participation in the application of the Treaty. "If by any mysterious influence of error," said the President, "America should not take the leading part in this new enterprise of concerted power, the world would experience one of those reversals of sentiment, one of those penetrating chills of reaction, which would lead to a universal cynicism, for if America goes back upon mankind, mankind has no other place to turn." But Mr. Keynes insisted that it was Europe that had gone back upon America, that the Treaty was a betrayal of American ideals, an economic absurdity, an instrument of systematic oppression and murder. Not content with presenting the statesmen of the Peace Conference with these amenities, he showered ridicule upon President Wilson. This was at a time when all hope of associating the United States in European reconstruction was hanging on the success of the President's efforts to have the Treaty accepted by the American people. His was already a losing battle; and in the thick of the fight, while Mr. Keynes was busy thus writing, he had finally broken down. It would seem that prudence recommended the familiar injunction "Do not shoot the pianist. . . ." But the sarcastic verve of Mr. Keynes swept on with irrepressible

gusto. Was it really possible to resist such a temptation? What a first-class "stunt" would be his "inside story" of the Conference! How the world would laugh at his sallies against the old Puritan of the White House! And so "the poor President" was pictured as a "blind and deaf Don Quixote," terrorized by Clemenceau or hypnotized by Mr. Lloyd George. Nothing could have better pleased the enemies of the President at home. In his plea for mercy to the beaten foe, Mr. Keynes was to appeal with success to the traditional British distaste for hitting a man when he is down. But what matter? the man who was now going down was a friend. The time was up. The cock was already crowing.

The Economic Consequences of the Peace appeared in the United States in January 1920. It had a phenomenal sale. "The truth is," said General Smuts many years later, "America wanted a reason for denying Wilson. The world wanted a scapegoat. At that opportune moment Keynes brought out his *Economic Consequences of the Peace*. There were a few pages about Wilson in it which exactly suited the policies of America and the world's mood. When I encouraged Keynes to write that book, I knew his views about the statesmen at Paris. But I did not expect a personal note in his book. I did not expect him to turn Wilson into a figure of fun. These few pages about Wilson in Keynes's book made an Aunt Sally of the noblest figure — perhaps the only noble figure — in the history of the war, and they led a fashion against Wilson that was adopted by the Intelligentsia of the day and is not yet past — the Intelligentsia (not the Intellectuals) — the people who, admiring only their own cleverness, despise real goodness, real thought, real wisdom. . . . Every paper I saw," added the General, "quoted the part about Wilson's bamboozlement. Wilson was already going down in America. In their hearts, the Americans wanted him to go down: they wanted to evade the duties he imposed on them. The book was absolutely to their purpose. It helped to finish Wilson, and it strengthened the Americans against the League."

Judging from the use made of Mr. Keynes's book during the debate over the Peace Treaty, it is hard to find fault with General Smut's comments. The book was seized by the President's opponents as a first-rate weapon in the fight then raging. It was quoted extensively as evidence of the infamous deeds committed at Paris, and in which America would not connive. On 10 February, Senator Borah read long extracts in the Senate; his comments could scarcely improve upon Mr. Keynes's text. "His contention," he said, "is that the German Treaty consigns continental Europe to perpetual famine and chronic revolution; that unless the Treaty is completely revised and rewritten, it must inevitably result that the economic system of Europe will be destroyed, which will result in the loss of millions of lives and in revolution after revolution, which necessarily follows when a people find themselves in the condition to which the people of Europe will be reduced. . . . When you think of the fact that they have lightly wrecked the entire economic system of an entire continent and reduced to starvation millions of people and perhaps prevented the world peace from coming at all in this decade, there is no language too severe for such men. . . . The Treaty in its consequences is a crime born of blind revenge and insatiable greed."

One month later, the Treaty was finally defeated. From that time on, the Keynesian picture was to remain implanted in the American mind. The horrors of Versailles became a veritable article of faith. They were used at every juncture to show that there was really no difference between the nations of Europe—that they were all equally revengeful, equally machiavellian, equally imperialistic; that the entry of America in the last war had been a ghastly mistake; and that the issue of any new one would be to her a matter of indifference, for an Allied victory would probably be no better than Versailles and a German victory could certainly be no worse. And thus, in sheer despair of a continent that would not be redeemed, America declared herself neutral: should war break out, she would be interested in neither party; all she would be interested in was keeping out. Whatever might happen in Europe, it was all the fault of Versailles.

* * *

A new Europe had come into shape, where "large units" dominated the scene; "an extraordinary episode in the economic progress of man" had begun. Would the great Powers rest in contentment? Would Peace be secure? But millions of subjects were still under alien domination. Hardly less than the Ottoman Empire, the Austro-Hungarian Monarchy was a composite of different races now agitating for a larger measure of autonomy, if not for independence proper. By far the largest group was made up of Slav peoples who looked to Russia, the "big brother," for support, as Russia looked to the *bratouchki* as a vehicle of influence in Central and Southern Europe. From the gradual disintegration of the Ottoman Empire either Russia or Austria-Hungary must profit, and with the impending rottenness of the Austro-Hungarian structure, this double process of dislocation would share its effects between Russia and Germany. "The key to the whole situation in East Europe,—and it is a fact which cannot be too clearly laid to heart at the present moment," wrote Sir Halford Mackinder in 1919, "is the German claim to dominance over the Slav." After the Austro-Prussian war of 1866, Mazzini had announced that the downfall of Turkey would be followed by the downfall of Austria; and in the very year of the Berlin Congress, when Russia's intervention in favour of the Slav subjects of Turkey had nearly brought about a war with the British Empire, the French historian Sorel had observed that once Europe came to believe the Eastern Question solved, the Austrian Question would inevitably arise. It was the Austrian question that precipitated the war in 1914; and in that very year the Irish question, that running sore of Britain's domestic politics, had brought the nation to the verge of civil war. In 1919, Mr. Keynes, who confessed candidly that "to become a European in his cares and outlook" was "for him a new experience," may no doubt be excused for having scolded the Council of Four because they bothered with such "unreal issues" as frontiers and sovereignties. No one can very well blame the good lady who found her cakes burning for thinking that King Alfred's preoccupations were unreal in the extreme. But it should not be very difficult to understand why, to the statesmen who sat down in 1919 to organize a world where the main causes of war would have been extirpated, the root of the trouble appeared as the problem of nationality.

Yet Mr. Keynes did not hesitate to accuse them of taking an irresponsible view of their duties. "The future life of Europe was not their concern; its means of livelihood was not their anxiety." "It is," he wrote, "an extraordinary fact that the fundamental economic problem of a Europe starving and disintegrating before their eyes, was the one question in which it was impossible to arouse the interest of the Four." For so serious a charge there must surely have been serious evidence; so it is somewhat disconcerting to find it propounded by one who had sat, as deputy for the Chancellor of the Exchequer, at the Supreme Economic Council. This body had been appointed in February 1919 on the initiative of President Wilson and had absorbed all the existing inter-Allied services already dealing with problems of finance, food, blockade, and raw materials. Its functions were "to examine such economic measures as shall be taken during the period of reconstruction after the War, so as to ensure (a) a due supply of materials and other commodities necessary for the restoration of the devastated areas; (b) the economic restoration of the countries which have suffered most from War; (c) the supply of neutral and ex-enemy countries without detriment to the supply of the needs of the Allied and Associated countries." Its mission was therefore entirely one of economic administration (such as the reorganization of European transport) and of assistance to the many parts of Europe threatened with starvation. In the performance of this task, its relief section, under Mr. Herbert Hoover distributed some 35,000,000 tons of commodities of every kind. But it was natural that the Council, whose agenda covered the whole settlement, not merely of Europe but of various other parts of the world as well, should not have devoted to that particular side of its task an undue proportion of its overcrowded time. After a long sitting, on 5 March, had been almost entirely occupied by the question of European relief, Lord Balfour observed that "it was unnecessary that every proposal of the Supreme Economic Council should be referred for sanction to the five Powers. The Economic Council had, he understood, executive authority within the terms of its reference." Very properly, the Supreme Council of the Allies delegated their responsibility in this sphere to the Economic Council. If any criticism should be directed at the Supreme Council's procedure, it would be that on the whole they were rather tempted to take too much into their own hands, and it is to be regretted, perhaps, that they did not in other provisional matters follow this wise attitude of discharging their executive and administrative duties upon some subordinate body.

Thus the alleged unconcern of the Four with these problems is not to be attributed to "empty and arid intrigue." The facts are there to show that the requirements of relief and rehabilitation had not been overlooked. But economic relief and rehabilitation would have been of small avail unless the uprooted peoples of Europe could know to what allegiance they were to belong in future — where they would stand, and whether they were to stand or to crouch. Under no other condition could Europe have gone back to work. That the statesmen of 1919 concerned themselves with political and territorial problems in the first place, rather than with direct economic administration, is slender proof that "the future life of Europe was not their concern." It proves only that they did not think it possible to set even economic recovery in train before Europe had been made again orderly and peaceful. And in view of the national passions with which Europe was ablaze, the problem was not a simple one.

For some of the forces that had been instrumental to the outbreak of the war were to assist the Allies in winning it. During the final assault against the Central Empires, the Allies had found in the insurrection of the Slav nations a powerful support; and only through the hazards of war were the extraordinary conditions manufactured that made it possible, in a moment unique in history, to look forward to a Europe of free nations. "Alas," wrote Clemenceau ten years later, "we must have the courage to say that our programme, when we entered the War, was not one of liberation! . . . We had started as allies of the Russian oppressors of Poland, with the Polish soldiers of Silesia and Galicia fighting against us. By the collapse of military Russia Poland found herself suddenly set free and recreated, and then all over Europe oppressed peoples raised their heads, and our war of national defence was transformed by force of events into a war of liberation. . . . A Europe founded upon right . . . instead of a dismembered Europe, was a fine dramatic turn of events."

Now if any maxim could have summed up the programme brought to Europe by President Wilson, it would surely be that the principle of self-determination must henceforward prevail over that of the balance of power. "An evident principle," he had explained in his Fourteen Points speech, "runs throughout the whole program I have outlined. It is the principle of justice to all peoples and nationalities, and their right to live on equal terms of liberty and safety with one another, whether they be strong or weak." "Peoples and provinces," he had said a little later, "are not to be bartered about from sovereignty to sovereignty as if they were mere chattels and pawns of a game, even the great game, now forever discredited, of the balance of power." No resolution could have been implanted in the mind of the President (or, for that matter, of Mr. Lloyd George) more firmly than that the peace of the world should never again be at the mercy of the ferment of national irredentism. What they did not perhaps perceive was that whenever this ferment had succeeded in destroying the peace of Europe, it had done so by first upsetting the balance of power; and that without the firm establishment of such a balance, the "equal rights" of weak nations would sooner or later wither away before the unequal forces of the strong.

The difficulties that followed the creation of so many independent states have induced a growing amount of reflection over the merits of self-determination — merits, it was widely believed in 1919 and after, that could be questioned only for unavowably reactionary motives. Thus could Mr. Keynes picture Clemenceau as paying lip-service, for diplomatic reasons "to the 'ideals' of foolish Americans and hypocritical Englishmen," but at the same time refusing to believe that there was "any sense in the principle of self-determination except as an ingenious formula for rearranging the balance of power in one's own interests." Whether or not this was Clemenceau's real view, others beside him were also to express some startling strictures at the time. "When the President talks of 'self-determination'," wrote Mr. Robert Lansing in December 1918, "what unit has he in mind? Does he mean a race, a territorial area, or a community? Without a definite unit which is practical, application of this principle is dangerous to peace and stability. . . . The phrase is simply loaded with dynamite. It will raise hopes which can never be realized. It will, I fear, cost thousands of lives. In the end, it is bound to be discredited, to be called the dream of an idealist who failed to realize the dangers until too late to check those who attempt to put this principle in force. What a calamity that the phrase was ever uttered! What misery it will cause!"

It is worth while observing, in view of the widespread legend of the Conference as a combat between American idealism and European cynicism, that one of the most realistic criticisms of self-determination made at the time came, not from some Machiavellian politician of the Old World, but from an American Secretary of State.

These reservations have been resumed in recent times on a more systematic scale. Thus Professor E. H. Carr, in a book that has gained wide currency, has stressed in stimulating manner the difference between self-determination, understood as a subjective right, based upon the desire "by a group of people of reasonable size" to constitute a state, and nationality, derived from such objective characteristics as "differences of physical type, or . . . differences of language, culture and tradition." There is, he writes, "a potential incongruity between nationality and self-determination" which was, he asserts, "ignored by the peacemakers" "who were unconscious of any discrepancy or indeed any distinction" between the two. This confusion, however, is to be explained by the fact that the two did practically coincide in Western Europe and in most of the overseas countries whose civilization was derived from Western Europe. But in Eastern Europe, things were no longer so simple. Here, continues Professor Carr, *language* was not the criterion of subjective will to form a state, as was shown by such plebiscites as Allenstein and Marienwerder, where Polish-speaking inhabitants voted for Germany, or at Klagenfurt, where Slovene-speaking inhabitants voted for Austria. In short, with the exception of the clauses providing for plebiscites, nationality rather than self-determination was the guiding principle of the Conference.

Such a conflict could not have been solved in favour of either of the two alleged principles alone without uprooting the very lives of the peoples whom the Conference was endeavouring to resettle. Brought to its ultimate logic, self-determination would have meant not merely *universal* plebiscites, but *permanent* plebiscites. For why should

the final shape of a nation be fixed according to what its people thought in 1919? Renan had described the life of a truly united nation as "a plebiscite of every day." But he would have been first to add that it could not apply literally to nations in becoming, until time, tradition, prescription, had made a living reality of "the soul, the spiritual principle" without which a nation could not exist. "To have common glories in the past, a common will in the present; to have accomplished great things together, and to want to accomplish more in the future: these are the essential conditions that make a people. . . ." No one in 1919 suggested that all Europe should be submitted to plebiscites, and even the most fervent supporters of self-determination could understand the dangers of anarchy that would follow if it were carried to the extreme. There was nothing then that could differentiate the right of self-determination from the "right" to secession; and all the world could remember that the President who had now made himself the champion of self-determination was the successor of another President who had fought the most terrible war in the history of his country to save it from that very peril. A literal view of the principle would have meant that unless the whole territorial structure of Europe was determined by plebiscites, the Wilsonian programme would be violated.

No one present at the Conference ever took this view — not even President Wilson. In the earliest stages of the Conference, and before Mr. Lloyd George could have had any reasonable time to "bamboozle" him, he made it clear that the adjustment of his principles to concrete cases could not be effected on such simplified lines. "If," he declared on 30 January, "a map of Europe were produced showing the limits of the territories to be created, based on historical, racial and economic facts, the Great Powers could then sit down to consider those suggestions and give weight to those points of view, such as expediency, natural antagonisms, etc., which played no part in scholarly wisdom." Time and again, as such difficulties came up for solution, it was admitted that some compromise was necessary. "It would in many parts of the world," said Lord Balfour, "be necessary to modify the ethnological principle by geographical and economic considerations. It had seemed to him that confusion would be increased and difficulties doubled by first offering votes to the population, and after recording the resulting of their votes, disregarding it. Would it not be better to say beforehand that there were certain considerations which must outweigh national sentiments, rather than by consulting the latter to make it almost impossible to allege the former?" What Professor Carr ascribes to a confusion between self-determination and nationality was rather the tacit admission that the conflict could not be solved in favour of either one alone of the two. Furthermore, the fact that *language* is no sufficient criterion of the will to form a nation is the proof, not that self-determination does not coincide with nationality, but merely that nationality does not coincide with language.

Like those of any individual, the wants of a nation are multiple, and they are not always compatible. The mere wish of every "national group" to form an independent state was hardly a sufficient basis for its future national existence. The peoples "concerned" did not only want to belong to this or that nation; they also insisted that the nation to which they belonged should be strong, prosperous, and secure.

The economic consequences of territorial changes have been a source of frequent misunderstanding. In a famous book Sir Norman Angell once endeavoured to dispel some of them by demonstrating that under conditions of modern capitalism, private property, and free enterprise, territorial aggrandizement did not in itself enrich a conquering nation. As long as the property rights of the conquered were respected (and they could not fail to be), the conqueror gained in territory and population, but not in wealth; conversely, the people remaining in the mutilated country was not directly impoverished. We have learned to-day that

wholesale expropriation and extermination have made the profits of totalitarianism something more than a "Great Illusion"; but in view of the humane attitude of the victors in 1919, Sir Norman's conclusions had then acquired a very practical significance.

Yet even under this now obsolete method of territorial transfers, the presence of valuable economic resources is not a matter of indifference to the nation that is to gain or lose them. The nation *as a whole* will be richer as a consequence of the accretion of a rich population. National finance is strengthened by the application of taxation to the richer regions; and even in the absence of the multifarious forms of state control which may be used to turn the new resources into a literally national asset, their inclusion within the country's boundaries will in itself increase national wealth, were it merely because the population can migrate to the richer area without losing its national character. For all these reasons, "economic considerations" were invoked during the Conference to support various claims for territorial annexation.

Now the removal of a political boundary between two regions may help to improve the economic welfare of both, regardless of considerations of aggregate economic *power*, since it also removes the *pretext* for putting obstacles to the free play of those forces which will naturally operate the most efficient geographical location of the factors of production. But the existence of a political boundary does not *by itself* render these transformations impossible or even more difficult. Even *within* one country, the produce of a region is being *exchanged* against that of another; all that a new boundary will do will be to substitute international for interregional trade — but not to suppress trade altogether. Thus, as Mr. Keynes remarked, political boundaries would be of little consequence to the economic intercourse in a régime of Free Trade. But, he added, "men have devised ways to impoverish . . . one another"; and "calculating on the present passions and impulses of European capitalistic society," Europe's output would be in each case "diminished by a new political frontier (which sentiment and historic justice require), because nationalism and private interest are thus allowed to impose a new economic frontier along the same lines."

What has happened since would seem enough to confirm amply the pertinence of this remark. Everywhere tariff barriers, reinforced with all manner of contrivances designed to promote economic self-sufficiency, have contributed to hamper the fullest economic development of Europe and of the rest of the world. But the conclusion drawn by Mr. Keynes was hardly legitimate: if frontiers were to grow whereever political frontiers were drawn, the fault lay with "the present passions and impulses of European capitalistic society," and not with the Peace Treaty. The idea that "natural economic regions" should not be "arbitrarily" partitioned may seem at first glance a highly reasonable one; but what is a "natural economic region?" If complete self-sufficiency is being aimed at, where are the limits at which territorial extension will stop? No European nation could be economically self-sufficient, and not even the inclusion of all in one single European unit could have made them so. Had Mr. Keynes's complaints about the economic evils of political frontiers been consistent, they would not have justified his criticism of the changes wrought by the Treaty in *existing* frontiers — they would, rather, have justified his asking for their universal abolition — unless the "Economic Eldorado" of pre-war days which he described in his opening chapter represented in his eyes such an acme of universal bliss as to render abhorrent any change in the political *status quo* of 1914. But Mr. Keynes, who, as we shall see, had severe remarks to offer about the impracticability of restoring Europe to 1870, did not appear to realize that it would be just as difficult to restore it even approximately to 1914.

And yet, considerable ingenuity was spent at the Conference in efforts to provide the new states with sufficient economic resources to make a reality of their political independence. Mr. Harold Nicolson has complained of the difficulties raised by such problems: "No guidance," he writes, "was . . . given us as to the inevitable conflict between 'self determination' and 'economics.' The French were always insisting that our main duty was to render the New States what they called *viables,* or in other words to provide them with those essentials of security, transport, and economic resources without which they would be unable to establish their independence. We were never told how far we were to accept this argument." Perhaps the reason was that it was actually impossible to lay down hard and fast rules by the mere economic standard.

A characteristic instance of such problems is provided by the case of the German-speaking parts of Bohemia. When he presented it before the Supreme Council, Dr. Beneš made a long plea for the maintenance of the existing frontier between Germany and the Bohemian part of Austria-Hungary. This would, admittedly, include a minority of German character in the new Czechoslovakia; a number of arguments, historical and political, were nevertheless given in favour of this solution. "The best argument, however," added Dr. Beneš, "on which to establish the rights of the Czechs was of an economic order. The Czecho-German parts of Bohemia contained nearly the whole of the industries of the country. Bohemia as a whole was the strongest industrial portion of Austria-Hungary. . . . Without the peripheral areas, Bohemia could not live. The center of the country was agricultural, and the two parts were so interdependent that neither could exist without the other. If the Germans were to be given the outer rim of Bohemia they would also possess the hinterland." Accordingly, and almost without discussion, it was decided that the frontier between Bohemia and Germany would remain as it was in 1914. A minority of some three million German-speaking people was included in Czechoslovakia. Here was clear instance where "economic considerations" had prevailed over the strictest application of the principle of self-determination. Perhaps for this very reason, Mr. Keynes was satisfied with the solution arrived at, for he made no critical reference to it. And yet it was precisely the problem of the Sudeten Germans that brought Europe to the brink of war in September 1938. Thus, even when food, coal, and transport were given their due share of attention, frontiers and sovereignties would still be inviting trouble.

Now the choice between economic and political advantage cannot be decided once for all, and calls for more than a judgment of fact, as it must rest, in the last resort, upon a choice of values. Long before Herman Goering's notorious remark about the advantage of guns over butter, Adam Smith, for one, had expressed with the sweet simplicity of his age the opinion that defense was of much more importance than opulence. But there is no *demonstrable* reason in the world why any one should not prefer one to the other, and swap (whenever he finds it practicable) freedom for prosperity. After all, the earliest transaction of this type ever recorded could never have taken place if Esau had not *preferred* the pottage. For a long time the popular view has been that it was not he who had ultimately made the best out of that bargain; but this is now probably little else than a canting old-fashioned prejudice, in an age that takes for granted the "primacy of economics over politics" — or indeed, over anything else. In 1919, the days were at hand when Mr. Ford would explain that what is economically right is also morally right; and to proclaim that the Peace Treaty was economically wrong was enough already to damn it as a whole. The times foreseen by Burke were there: the age of economists and calculators had truly come.

*   *   *

"Two rival schemes for the future polity of the world took the field — the Fourteen Points of the President, and the Carthagenian Peace of M. Clemenceau," wrote Mr. Keynes as he narrated this pathetic conflict of the forces of idealism and prog-ress against those of cynicism and reaction, ending in the final "collapse" of the man who had come to Europe as the bearer of the hopes so dear. The public at large has never since been able to shake off the spell cast by this fascinating and highly sensational story.

To the burning patriotism of Clemenceau, as well as to his uncanny charm, Mr. Keynes paid a deeply felt and moving tribute. His portrait of the old Tiger, who "had one illusion — France; and one disillusion — mankind, including Frenchmen" was masterly, and it is beyond anyone's power to excel it. But in addition, he charged Clemenceau — and with him, the whole of French policy — with the deliberate intention of *destroying* the German nation. "So far as possible . . . it was the policy of France to set the clock back and to undo what, since 1870, the progress of Germany had accomplished. By loss of territory and other measures her population was to be curtailed; but chiefly the economic system, upon which she depended for her new strength, the vast fabric built upon iron, coal, and transport, must be destroyed." Clemenceau's aim, he explained was "to weaken and destroy Germany in every possible way." Such a policy, he continued, was condemned, not merely by its inhumanity but by its impracticability. "My purpose in this book is to show that the Carthagenian Peace is not *practically* right or possible. . . . The clock cannot be set back. You cannot restore central Europe to 1870 without setting up such strains in the European structure and letting loose such human and spiritual forces as, pushing beyond frontiers and races, will overwhelm not only you and your 'guarantees,' but your institutions, and the existing order of your Society."

Now it may first be pointed out not only that it is quite possible to set a clock back, but also that when the clock is wrong it is often a very sensible thing to do. That, however, is not the essential point. The point is that only by acrobatic flight of historical fancy could a settlement that left Europe with a unified Germany and a decomposed Austria bear the reproach of restoring Central Europe to 1870, when things stood exactly the other way round. The point is that the economic power achieved by Germany between 1871 and 1914 had been greatly assisted by political unity; and that to "restore Central Europe in 1870" would have meant, first of all, undoing this unity.

A not negligible body of opinion in France had been urging that every opportunity of exploiting to this end whatever currents manifested themselves in Germany should be used to the full before coming to the conclusion that such a policy was not feasible; and as the Empire of the Hohenzollerns crumbled to pieces, several ominous symptoms had appeared under the cracked carapace. In Bavaria, an independent Republic had been proclaimed. In the Rhineland, a genuine feeling for the separation from Prussia was becoming increasingly evident. In Wurtemberg, in Baden, even in Saxony, allegiance to Berlin was rudely shaken. It is impossible to ascertain today to what lengths such forces might have carried the German States if they had received more attention in Allied quarters; but what is certain is that the amplitude they had reached was no better apprehended then than had been the true weakness of Germany before the conclusion of the Armistice.

It has been said that in June 1919, after Scheidemann had resigned rather than sign the Treaty, and when the German Government had but a few hours left to accept or reject the Peace terms, Bauer, the new Chancellor, was pressed by the German High Command to refuse his signature. At that moment a delegation from the Southern German States asked to be admitted. "If," they declared, "the Treaty is not signed, the Allied armies now waiting on the Rhine will march into Germany. We shall be the first to suffer invasion. Rather than submit to this, we shall make our own terms with the Allies and secede from the Reich."

So Europe had perhaps gone through one of those exceptional moments in history — moments that can sometimes be shaped, if seized by a quick and masterly hand, into an enduring future. There is a tide in the affairs of men . . . But to Clemenceau the Jacobin — who saw in the march of nations to unity one of those irreversible forces of modern times, and who remembered how, in spite of many lamentable illusions to the contrary, Saxons and Bavarians had all flocked to the colours in 1870, and joined Prussia in the common defence of the German fatherland, as well as in the common assault against France — the unity of Germany was an accomplished and final fact. In this sense, indeed, he was a man of 1870. If he refused to listen to the advocates of dissociation, it was not merely in acknowledgement of the opposition of his British and American colleagues — it was because such proposals, in his eyes, bore the mark of the reactionary, and because, at the bottom of his own political philosophy, there was indeed the conviction (which many of his critics did not fail to use as a reproach) that the "clock cannot be put back." "The question" he said to the French parliament, "was settled at the Conference almost before it had been presented."

Thus the Allies either did not know or would not see how perilous was the sea on which they were then afloat. The Treaty of Versailles was signed, and the unity of Germany preserved. And as the book that was to denounce his "Carthagenian Peace" was being written, Clemenceau, now engaged in the defence of his policy before parliament, was pleading that Germany *could not* be permanently destroyed.

"Today," he said, "we are masters. Nevertheless, if we want a conciliation in the interests of our children, of the future, we must use this superiority with a moderation sufficient but necessary to assure its duration. If we do this, Germany is disarmed. Yet, if we want Germany to pay Reparations, she will have to work. This is a problem that we cannot escape. To those Italian diplomats who will not understand that they must make friends of the Serbs and of the Slavs, that without this there can be no peace in Europe, I often say: 'Unite with them instead of making them your enemies.' I would almost say the same of the Germans. I do not want to run after their good will — I do not have the proper feelings for that. Still, sixty million people in the centre of Europe will take some room, especially when they are men of science, of method, who have shown, in industrial fields, the most brilliant qualities. Do we have an interest in denying it? Is it not truth? We have no right to forget it. . . . Unity, you see, is not in the protocols of diplomacy. . . . It is in the hearts of men."

The Treaty was ratified by parliament; but a few months later, Clemenceau was defeated at the Presidential election, and among the hostile votes, those expressing the resentment against the man "who had won the war and lost the peace" were not a few. It is but another of those familiar ironies of fate that Clemenceau, after ten years of scornful silence, spent the last months of his life answering those who had blamed him for having compromised the security of his country, and that he died almost pen in hand, justifying in a heart-rending book his refusal to dismember Germany. If it is contended that an excess of territorial divisions was the chief obstacle brought by the Treaty to the economic recovery of Europe, then, surely, some credit for having — in the teeth of bitter opposition, and at the cost of his downfall — opposed the political disruption of Germany should have gone to Clemenceau.

*   *   *

Mr. Keynes had predicted that the Reparation clauses could never be carried out. They never were. This outcome has earned him the glory of a prophet. It is perhaps fair that others should have some share of these laurels. Foch, for instance, had expressed his own opinion to M. Klotz in no equivocal terms: "With the Treaty you have just signed, sir," he said, "you can expect with certainty to be paid in monkey tricks." Neither was Foch alone, in France or elsewhere, in harbouring such misgivings.

Following events, as we have seen, confirmed several of the Marshal's presentiments. It would appear there here, too, his apprehensions were correct. Reparations were not outside the range of economic *possibility*. Had they been literally enforced, they would no doubt have put the screw on Germany up to the topmost pitch. For having suggested that Germany be *squeezed till the pips squeaked*, Sir Eric Geddes was exposed by Mr. Keynes to the superciliousness of a pharisaical posterity; it is too often forgotten that the man whose efficiency and drive had overcome, in the face of administrative prejudice, some of the deadliest "bottlenecks" of the war, and who himself had made Britain's own pips squeak in the process, was probably entitled to view the limits of financial possibility in a more sanguine light than many others. In fact, a large part of what appeared to increase the burden to such heavy proportions consisted in the provisions relating to interest, and the Treaty had given sufficient powers to the Commission to reduce the rate according to circumstances; Clemenceau himself had conceded that the Allies might have to forgo interest altogether. Reparations were not paid because Germany, as was quite natural, did not want to pay them, and — which was perhaps not *quite* so natural — the Allies showed themselves incapable or unwilling to take jointly the necessary measures which could have made Germany pay.

The whole question, therefore, boiled down to political expediency.

Now expediency, political or otherwise, is not a negligible factor in human affairs, and there would have been nothing dishonourable in taking account of it squarely in the making of the Peace. Thus, when the Draft Treaty came up for final reconsideration, it was to expediency that Mr. Lloyd George, at the meeting of the Imperial Cabinet, had explicitly drawn the attention of his colleagues. The terms imposed, he said, "must be expedient as well as just. Justice was a question which the Germans were at liberty to raise, but expediency was a matter for the Allies to consider and not the Germans. . . ." And almost at the same time, Mr. Hoover was raising the question at the meeting of the American delegation.

MR. HOOVER: Apart from all questions of justice, how far does the question of expediency come in?
PRESIDENT WILSON: In order to get them to sign, do you mean?
MR. HOOVER: In order to get them to sign. It strikes me that that is a more important thing than the question of justice or injustice, because the weighing of justice and injustice in these times is pretty difficult.
PRESIDENT WILSON: Yes, nobody can be sure they have made a just decision. But don't you think that if we regard the treaty as just, the argument of expediency ought not to govern, because, after all we must not give up what we fought for? We might have to fight for it again.
MR. HOOVER: But we look at expediency in many lights. It may be necessary to change the terms of the reparation in view of getting something, rather than to lose all. And it is not a question of justice; justice would require, as I see it, that they pay everything they have got or hope to get. But in order to obtain something, it may be expedient to do this, that and the other.

Expediency, therefore, could have been understood as requiring that Reparation demands should not be too heavy. In such a case, Mr. Keynes had shown a strong sense of political expediency in 1919. Yet, strangely enough, the criticism most frequently levelled against his book in early days was that it lacked all sense of political necessity. But, later on, it was his critics who were to be chaffed for their subservience to political opportunism and their disregard of economic laws. "One may," wrote Lord Stamp, several years afterwards, "distinguish political from economic wisdom by saying that the latter will and must ultimately prevail, but that it is too hard and unpalatable for a world that will not 'come off' its wishes until relentlessly pulled by the force of events. It may be political 'wisdom' to flatter the public mind with slightly weaker and weaker doses of what it likes and slightly stronger and

stronger doses of what it will have to get used to. . . . If that be the sense of political wisdom, then Keynes's book wholly lacked it." Clearly "political necessity" could have more than one meaning.

I have endeavoured, for my part, to show that the demands of the Treaty of Versailles were not economically impossible. Whether they were *politically practicable* is of course another question. It could be contended that the economic and financial achievements of wartime were no longer obtainable in peacetime; that it was *politically impossible* for the Allies to enforce these demands upon the German people. We have seen, for instance, that Mr. Keynes did not believe that the German Government would have the power to increase the length of the working day. He feared, in 1919, that excessive demands might provoke revolution in Central Europe. He explicitly declared that there were cases where "particular claims, however well founded in sentiment or in justice, must yield to sovereign expediency." And he claimed, a few years later, that neither the collection of War Debts nor the enforcement of Reparations was "serious politics" in the long run.

The Economic Consequences of the Peace, therefore, did not "wholly lack" a sense of "political wisdom." It was probably impolitic to run the risk of incurring Germany's resentment if one was not prepared to take the consequences. It was certainly impolitic to overlook the indisputable fact that Germany's nuisance value was greater than that of her victims. But then it is hard to see how this political wisdom on the international plane was very different, in moral essence, from (say) the subservience of politicians to the wrath of their electorates. It was only much later that "realism" was frankly invoked to justify the appeasement of Germany. But then Mr. Keynes protested that it was "to fraternize with what is vile."

In 1919, the Allied and Associated Powers, rightly or wrongly, had not believed that to compromise with justice would be an act of political wisdom. "Justice" they said in their Reply to the German delegation, "is the only possible basis for the settlement of the account of the terrible war. Justice is what the German delegation asks for and says that Germany has been promised. Justice is what Germany shall have. But it must be justice for all. There must be justice for the dead and wounded and for those who have been orphaned and bereaved that Europe might be freed from Prussian despotism. There must be justice for the peoples who now stagger under war debts which exceed £30,000,000,000 that liberty might be saved. There must be justice for those millions whose homes and land, ships and property German savagery has spoilated and destroyed.

"That is why the Allied and Associated Powers have insisted as a cardinal feature of the Treaty that Germany must undertake to make reparation to the very uttermost of her power; for reparation for wrongs inflicted is of the essence of justice. . . . Somebody must suffer for the consequences of the war. Is it to be Germany, or only the peoples she has wronged?

"Not to do justice to all concerned would only leave the world open to fresh calamities. If the German people themselves, or any other nation, are to be deterred from following the footsteps of Prussia, if mankind is to be lifted out of the belief that war for selfish ends is legitimate to any State, if the old era is to be left behind and nations as well as individuals are to be brought beneath the reign of law, even if there is to be an early reconciliation and *appeasement,** it will be because those responsible for concluding the war have had the courage to see that justice is not deflected for the sake of convenient peace."

But Mr. Keynes was not satisfied. "I cannot," he wrote, "leave this subject as though its just treatment wholly depended either in our pledges or on economic facts. The policy of reducing Germany to servitude for a generation, of degrading the lives of millions of human beings, and of depriving a whole nation of happiness should be abhor-

* Author's italics.

rent and detestable—abhorrent and detestable, even if it were possible, even if it enriched ourselves, even if it did not sow the decay of the whole civilized life of Europe. Some preach it in the name of Justice. In the great events of man's history, in the unwinding of the complex fate of nations Justice is not so simple. And if it were, nations are not authorized, by religion or by natural morals, to visit on the children of their enemies the misdoings of parents or of rulers." Amen. But what was to be *the alternative?* Could Mr. Keynes tell us *how* the innocent was to be saved? *Delicta majorum immeritus lues.* . . . What happened was that the misdoings of a nation were visited on the children of its victims.

*   *   *

Now the present book was never intended as an apologia for the Treaty of Versailles; but while the economic defects of that settlement were, for the most part, illusory or exaggerated, the present writer shares the opinion of those who have maintained that the political defects were the really decisive ones. It may have been a mistake, from the economic point of view, to allow or even encourage the break-up of the Danubian Monarchy into several sovereign states; but these states were always free, had they found it to their interest, to organize themselves into some sort of economic federation, and in so far as they failed to do this, the economic loss thus caused has been sustained primarily by themselves. How much more serious to the rest of the world, on the other hand, have been the *political* consequences of the division of Central and South-Eastern Europe! There, as has in fact frequently been pointed out, lay the cardinal vice of the system—in the constitution of a Europe where a strong and centralized Germany of some 70 millions remained surrounded by a string of small states, who had to rely for the preservation of their independence upon the assistance of faraway Powers; to put it shortly, in the failure, and one might almost say in the deliberate failure, to establish a true *balance of power*.

For Wilson himself, intent though he was upon the rejection of this type of diplomatic system, had foreseen that the Europe which he had thus left, largely by his own doing, was not one that could be expected to stand by itself — that without the support of outside Powers, Germany would yet have her will upon it. "All the nations that Germany meant to crush and reduce to the status of tools in her own hands have been redeemed by this war," he had explained, "and given the guarantee of the strongest nations of the world that nobody shall invade their liberty again. If you do not want to give them that guarantee, then you make it certain that . . . the attempt will be made again, and if another war starts like this one, are you going to keep out of it?" Now the League of Nations was designed to ensure precisely this kind of support. But the Powers concerned proved themselves unwilling, undecided, or unprepared to face their responsibilities in time. The truth is, that the spirit in which the League had been conceived presumed too much of them. As has been well said, "it was not the League that failed, but the nations." And if Wilson was guilty of one illusion, that illusion was mankind.

THE DILEMMA OF REPARATIONS— AN AMERICAN VIEW

JOHN FOSTER DULLES

As counsel to the American Commission to Negotiate Peace and a member of both the Reparations Commission and the Supreme Economic Council, John Foster Dulles played a vital role in formulating the economic terms of the German peace treaty. His account, written as a foreword to Philip M. Burnett's study of *Reparation at the Paris Peace Conference*, raises a number of significant questions concerning American attitudes toward Germany's ability to discharge her reparations obligations, and the War Guilt clause which furnished the legal basis for reparations.

I T IS good that significant events of the past should be adequately recorded. Only through their study can mankind acquire the wisdom which will permit it to deal more competently with the problems of the future.

The present volumes and their analysis by Mr. Philip M. Burnett constitute an important historical contribution. Since, however, the significance of this documentary material depends, to some extent, on extraneous circumstances, I have gladly accepted the invitation to make a few prefatory remarks.

It is first to be borne in mind that the material here presented is derived primarily from American sources. There are included many papers which reflect ideas and reasoning of the American delegates as formulated for their own internal consideration and

From John Foster Dulles, "Foreword," in Philip M. Burnett, *Reparation at the Paris Peace Conference* (New York, 1940), vol. I, pp. v–xiv. Reprinted by permission of Columbia University Press.

which were never brought to the attention of the delegates of other nationalities. In the case of informal and confidential meetings between delegates of the principal powers, the record here presented consists only of the notes made by one of the American participants. For such reasons it is inevitable that the American viewpoint should predominate and be more adequately expressed. It is to be hoped that other countries, particularly England and France, will arrange a comparable publication of their documentary material. Only thus will it be possible to obtain a balanced picture of what occurred and an accurate perception of the different viewpoints.

While a publication of English and French papers would permit their positions to be more sympathetically understood, it would probably not serve to reverse the verdict of history that on the major controversial issues the American position was the most sound. The American estimates of Germany's capacity to pay were more conservative and much less inaccurate than those put forward by other delegations. The exclusion of "war costs" was both legally and morally right and practically indispensable to preventing the reparation charge from becoming a grotesque figure. The interpretation of "damage to civilians" to include pensions and separation allowances merely added an uncollectable sum at the cost of undermining the moral foundation of reparation which otherwise would have been limited to items for which, in substance, Germany admitted liability. The postponement for two years of a fixation of the total liability may have made possible greater precision, but it was a precision which had only theoretical value, and the procedure retarded for two vital years the serious beginning of postwar reconstruction. All of this would now be generally conceded.

It is of course possible that the French and perhaps even the British, looked upon the reparation liability not as a means of financial relief to themselves but rather as an instrumentality for effecting the financial and economic ruin of Germany. If so, their views as expressed at the Peace Conference must be appraised by different standards. What then appeared to be misjudgments of financial and economic possibilities would have been part of an ulterior project in which they succeeded — at least temporarily. The real objectives of France and England cannot be known until there is a publication of French and English documents comparable with that here made of the confidential records of the American delegation. It is my personal belief that both the British and French reparation delegates were actuated by an honest desire to collect from Germany, although the French Government may have felt that overestimate of the economic and financial possibilities would not involve serious consequences for France, since there would then be compensating political advantages.

If, however, the judgments of the American delegates appear in retrospect to have been sounder than those of others, this should not be taken to prove that the Americans possessed superior moral or intellectual qualities. It proves rather that disinterested judgment is better than judgment which is inextricably intertwined with political considerations and considerations of self-interest. It is to be recalled that the United States sought no part in reparation and that reparation was not a political or popular issue with the American people. Therefore the American Commission at the Peace Conference could and did handle reparation purely as an issue to be dealt with on its merits. The problem was turned over to a group selected for their proven competence in economic and financial matters, with no instructions except to endeavor to secure the maximum reparation which, in accordance with their judgment, was compatible, on the one hand, with the Pre-Armistice Agreement, and, on the other hand, with economic possibilities. Mr. Vance C. McCormick had been Chairman of the War Trade Board from its inception. Mr. Bernard M. Baruch had similarly served as Chairman of the War Industries Board. Mr. Thomas W. Lamont and Mr. Norman

H. Davis had had wide experience in matters of international finance. These four functioned in complete harmony and constituted a highly effective unit. The freedom of action accorded them is illustrated by the fact that on only three occasions did they find it necessary to consult President Wilson with reference to major substantive issues. The first such occasion was at the inception of the Conference. A memorandum had then been drafted outlining the basic position which the American delegates proposed to take with reference to the principles governing reparation demands. This was submitted to the President, was initialed by him without change, and thereupon became the basic charter in accordance with which the American delegates guided their action. A second occasion arose when there developed a fundamental difference of opinion between the American delegates and those of the Allied powers with reference to the limiting effect of the Pre-Armistice Agreement. When the American delegates were unable, by themselves, to make further progress, they submitted the issue to the President — then on the S. S. "George Washington" — and sought his instructions. He responded with an affirmance of the original American position which was so incisive that it was no longer combated — at least frontally — by the other delegations. At a later stage of the Conference the question of including pensions and separation allowances was submitted to the President. He then overruled the judgment of his delegates, feeling that the point was debatable and should be conceded to secure that prompt accord on the Conditions of Peace which then seemed imperative. Doubtless on this subject, as on others, he relied upon the "revision" section (Article 19) of the League Covenant as a future corrective.

There were, of course, many phases of the reparation negotiations as to which the President was informed and consulted but, broadly speaking, the American reparation delegates functioned on their own responsibility and they were wholly free of political considerations.

The status of the American group contrasted markedly with that of the other reparation delegates. In the case of England, France, and Belgium reparation was the issue of the Conference upon which public opinion was most aroused. Thus, major decisions had to be carefully studied by the political heads of these States from the standpoint of the popular reaction to be expected therefrom. The British and French delegations comprised both financial and economic experts of independence and those who primarily reflected the domestic political strategy of their government. Thus the British delegation included Professor Maynard Keynes, who functioned as an independent Treasury expert, and Lord Cunliffe, Lord Sumner, and Prime Minister Hughes of Australia, who, on major issues, generally reflected the political viewpoint. The French group included Monsieur Georges Jouasset, a Treasury expert, and Ministers Klotz and Lebrun who were largely concerned with the political implications of what they did. Monsieur Loucheur combined political astuteness with some appreciation of economic possibilities.

It was doubtless inevitable that public opinion, so deeply aroused, should intrude into the conference room. But this fact and its implications prevented the British and French delegations from functioning with that independence of judgment and internal solidarity which characterized the American group.

There are certain other considerations which should be borne in mind in appraising the work of the reparation delegates.

The reparation section of the Conference was functioning in virtual ignorance of the concurrent work and decisions of other sections. While the reparation terms were being formulated, the reparation delegates did not know what territorial concessions would be required of Germany or what dispositions would be made of German colonies. While perhaps the colonies were of only minor importance in relation to capacity to pay, the same could not be said of coal and iron and of population in Germany proper. In the case of the American group there was, through Mr. Baruch, some liaison between those working on the reparation part and those working on the economic part of the Treaty. But the proceedings were so largely concurrent and the separate tasks were so engrossing of time and attention that the reparation group had to function with but inadequate knowledge of the trade possibilities which the Treaty would leave open to Germany. They were likewise uncertain as to the ultimate disposition which the Allied and Associated Powers would make of the foreign investments of German subjects which had been seized as a war measure.

That this should have been so was obviously a serious procedural defect, but one which, under the circumstances, it would have been difficult to rectify. Reappraisal of the Conditions of Peace as a whole, once they were brought together, was deemed impracticable because the provisions of each part of the Conditions of Peace reflected a balanced series of compromises and to have reopened any important number of provisions would have led by gradual progression to a reopening of the whole and there would have been a further long delay in consummating a peace which the world impatiently demanded. From the standpoint of perfection and of fairness it would doubtless have been better to negotiate a series of treaties dealing first with the more urgent and then with the less urgent problems. This procedure was considered but dismissed because of political and military considerations which seemed to require that the Conditions of Peace should be a single document, to be accepted or rejected as a whole.

Another consideration of importance was the ignorance of the delegates as to the procedure to be followed vis-à-vis the German delegates. As events turned out there was no personal contact with the German delegates for the purpose of discussion and negotiation. The Conference was one on the "Conditions of Peace"; there was, properly speaking, no "Peace Conference." The Conditions of Peace, once formulated, were submitted in writing, and written observations within a short time limit were the only German comment permitted. In practical effect the Conditions of Peace constituted an inflexible ultimatum. This, however, was not foreseen during the stages of the Conference when the reparation clauses were already assuming definitive form. It was then still assumed that there would be a conference with the German delegation and that their viewpoint, as then expressed, would be given serious consideration and that important changes might result therefrom. Thus no delegation, including the American, felt that there devolved upon it a primary duty to press to finality considerations with which the German delegation was primarily concerned and with respect to which it would be the natural and most effective exponent.

When the German written observations were received, the American delegates renewed, vigorously, their earlier efforts to secure a fixed liability of rational dimensions. But this effort failed for the same reasons that had dictated the procedure of submission to the Germans. The unity of the Allied and Associated Powers with respect to Conditions of Peace had been so difficult to achieve, and was of so fragile a nature, that it was feared it could not withstand the shock of reviewing the reparation part of the Treaty. Thus what was originally conceived of as a basis of discussion became without discussion the Treaty terms.

The documents here made public will bring to light, as never before, the extreme difficulty of securing agreement on Conditions of Peace. It was the judgment of the time that it was of paramount importance that unity between the Allied and Associated Powers should be preserved until the Treaty was accepted by Germany. If posterity accepts that judgment, it will excuse concessions of substance and form and the adoption of procedures which otherwise cannot but be condemned.

The student of psychology will find in these documents much of interest. There can be traced the processes by which disagreement was converted into agreement. These processes involved in varying degrees persuasion, concession, compromise, and the use of language sufficiently ambiguous to lend itself to either of two conflicting interpretations. The operation of different national characteristics can be traced. Perhaps most conspicuous in this respect was the disposition of the English and Americans to deal promptly and practically with the problem, even at the sacrifice of theoretical perfection. The French on the other hand were disposed to proceed by establishing certain broad principles as premises and then developing the logical consequences thereof by slow steps, each meticulously accurate. These contrasting attitudes became particularly apparent in the discussions relative to fixing in the Treaty itself a figure of damage.

While the Anglo-Saxon approach tended generally to be that of the "rough and ready" variety in contrast to the Latin disposition toward logical development and scientifically accurate application, there appears to have been less divergence than might have been expected on account of the different legal conceptions of the Common Law and of the Civil Law.

It is interesting to observe the difference between Lord Sumner, the advocate, arguing for "war costs" and pensions as instructed by his principal, Mr. Lloyd George, and Lord Sumner as chairman of the First Subcommittee (Categories of Damage), in which capacity his pre-eminent judicial qualities were afforded some scope.

The procedure, as between the Allied and Associated Powers, is also worthy of consideration. It was originally assumed that the reparation terms of the Treaty would be evolved through a group large enough to include representatives of all the powers substantially concerned, including the new Succession States. The size of the resultant group was, however, such as to necessitate the adoption by that group of formal methods. What might have been informal remarks and discussion took the form of prepared speeches, and oratory tended to replace simplicity and succinctness. The delegates of minor powers felt constrained to make speeches "for the record" and for home consumption. Much time was consumed by interpreters.

Such procedure continued until it demonstrably became impracticable and had to be replaced. Even then there was never any formal abandonment of the reparation section as originally constituted, but it and its subcommittees met less and less frequently, and such meetings as occurred became more perfunctory. Concurrently there occurred informal and confidential meetings of representatives of the three or four Great Powers, that is, Great Britain, France, the United States, and, part of the time, Italy. Belgium was also heard in confidential discussion with respect to her special position as a neutralized state.

Only through such confidential and intimate talks between representatives of the dominant powers did it become possible to make practical progress toward agreement, and the agreements thus arrived at had to be accepted by the lesser powers with as little opportunity for debate and discussion as was accorded Germany. Of course, their interest was secondary and where they were primarily concerned, as with the question of the responsibility of the Succession States for a part of the reparation liability of the enemy states, they were given an adequate hearing. This matter, for example, was dealt with by informal discussion largely between an American chosen to represent the viewpoint of the principal Allied Powers and Dr. Beneš of Czechoslovakia as spokesman for the Succession States.

The record clearly evidences the advantages of informal discussion by a few as against more formal procedures.

Analysis of the documents shows that the participants suffered from "blind spots." Of these the most important is that illustrated by the "war guilt" provision (Article 231). In the light of subsequent developments it may be that this article was the most important single article in the Treaty. Thereby, in German eyes, Germany was branded with moral guilt for the World War, and the German people, under threat of wholesale starvation and military devastation, were compelled to accept this verdict as true. It was the revulsion of the German people from this article of the Treaty, which, above all else, laid the foundation for the Germany which we see today. There was thus created a sense of injustice and a reaction against the imputed moral inferiority which was so intense as easily to lend itself to capitalization by leaders who were adept at arousing and directing human emotion. The significance of Article 231 was not adequately perceived by the reparation delegates or apparently by their Chiefs of State. The article emerged as an attempted compromise of the American viewpoint and that of the Allied Powers with respect to Germany's liability for "war costs." The Allies had, as we have noted, reluctantly acquiesced in the stand of President Wilson and the American delegation that Germany's contractual liability for reparation should be deemed limited by the Pre-Armistice Agreement and that this did not contemplate liability for "war costs." But while the Allies were prepared to concede that the Treaty should embody the *consequences* of such acquiescence on their part, they were not willing, doubtless for political reasons, that the Treaty should record the fact that by the Pre-Armistice Agreement they had waived that right to "integral" reparation which their people demanded. The British and French were thus insistent that the Treaty should consecrate their right to full reparation and excuse the exaction of only a part thereof on the ground of Germany's limited capacity to pay. In view of the extreme difficulty encountered in securing Allied acceptance of any limitation flowing from the Pre-Armistice Agreement, the American delegates were disposed to accept

a compromise in form and Article 231 was the expression of that compromise.

So intent were the American, British, and French delegates upon finding words that would compromise their own differences, so swayed were they by emotion against Germany, that the permanent effect upon Germany was not adequately perceived or considered. The reparation delegates had never been charged with the problem of war responsibility, which had been entrusted to another section of the Conference. They had no thought of consciously trespassing upon the work of the "Penalties" section. In their own minds they were merely finding a formula for solving different opinions as to Germany's theoretical liability for reparation. It came therefore as a surprise when German observations on the Conditions of Peace showed that this section could plausibly be, and in fact was, considered to be a historical judgment of "war guilt." The Treaty terms had by then become so generally known that modification of Article 231 was politically impossible and the reply of the Allied and Associated Powers to the German observations may have completed the metamorphosis of Article 231 from that which had originally been in the minds of the draughtsmen. It can thus be said that the profound significance of this article of the Treaty came about through accident, rather than design.

If through inadvertence the draughtsmen of the reparation clauses contributed largely toward a German psychology which has changed the political complexion of much of the world, so through lack of prescience they set up a force which has contributed to a profound change in the commercial and financial structure of the world. There had developed in the period before the war an elaborate system of international credit, and of balancing gold shipments, whereby the exchange of goods and services and the making of foreign investments were facilitated. The reparation possibilities were largely predicated upon the continuance of this system and assumed that reparation payments, over and above the specified deliveries in kind, would be made possible by credit operations such as the sale of German bonds. Thereby, it was assumed, reparation could be permanently absorbed into an expanded world credit structure and there could be an indefinite postponement of the problem of actually transferring goods or services in payment of this portion of reparation.

This conception might have been realizable if it had been held to modest limits. But the magnitude of the reparation payments demanded of Germany under the Treaty and under the implementing terms of the Dawes and Young Plans — particularly the latter — placed undue strain upon credit possibilities. Largely on this account there has been a widespread collapse of the entire prewar system of financing international movements of goods and services and investments. The prewar gold system has collapsed and a large part of the world functions in terms of closed national economies where international dealings are mostly restricted to barter transactions.

It is safe to say that none of the delegates at the Peace Conference foresaw adequately these possible developments or appraised narrowly enough the possibilities of credit. The American delegates did from time to time emphasize that reparation could in the long run be paid only by a transfer of goods and services. They took what they thought were necessary and adequate steps to set up a control over credit operations, realizing that the United States would be the principle source of credit. Thus they provided that for a commercialization of German reparation bonds *unanimous* consent of the Reparation Commission was required. This control did not, however, prove adequate. The United States never became an official member of the Reparation Commission and, in any event, the control thus provided might not have proved sufficiently broad. It could doubtless have been evaded by the system which actually developed, whereby reparation payments were for several years financed not by the sale of German government bonds but by the sale of bonds of German states, municipalities, and private corporations which turned over to the Reichsbank the foreign exchange resulting from their external loans. As to such credit operations no control was imposed either under the Treaty or under the subsequent Dawes and Young Plans.

It is useful periodically to pause and to study the sources from which evil and misfortune have flowed. It is easy when we do so to draw the conclusion that those who then played important parts on the world's stage were blind and stupid. Such a conclusion is warranted, but it is unimportant. What is important is to find the reasons for that blindness and stupidity which are now apparent. This, I think, cannot be adequately explained in terms merely of individual deficiencies. Rather it seems consequent upon operation of certain general principles. There are usually blindness and inadequate perception when emotion becomes the directive of human action. We usually turn out to have been stupid when we have attempted an artificial and extensive control over economic forces which we but vaguely understand.

The scope of what man can usefully attempt is constantly restricted by his lack of knowledge, and by moods which render unavailing that little knowledge which he does possess. The historical genesis of German reparation can serve as a lesson in this respect.

GREAT BRITAIN, FRANCE, AND THE EASTERN FRONTIERS OF GERMANY

W. M. JORDAN

As in the case of reparations, French and British views on redrawing Germany's eastern frontiers differed widely. These inter-Allied differences arose as much from a divergence of attitudes toward Germany and attempts to reconcile the principles of "national self-determination" and "economic viability" as from differing conceptions of the future European balance of power. Equally at stake were questions of German territorial integrity, Polish territorial and economic viability, and French conceptions of military security. After six years of intensive study, the British scholar, W. M. Jordan, under auspices of the Royal Institute of International Affairs, published in 1943 a monograph on *Great Britain, France and the German Problem 1918–1939*, which ranks as one of the most distinguished contributions to the history of interwar diplomacy. The student is urged most particularly to compare the French and British positions on Germany's eastern frontiers with that of Hitler.

T HE GREAT WAR resulted in the breakdown of the three great empires which had in 1914 dominated eastern and central Europe. From their ruins emerged the small national states whose existence was consecrated by the Treaties of Versailles, Saint-Germain, and Trianon. It is beyond the competence of the writer to explore the many political and economic problems to which this reorganization of the European states system gave rise. An adequate study would involve prolonged research. It is, therefore, in a somewhat tentative spirit that questions relating to eastern and central Europe are taken up in this chapter. No comprehensive survey is here proposed: nothing more is attempted than a sketch of the general trends of British and French policy toward the eastern neighbors of Germany.

For twenty years it has been widely regarded as the principal merit of the European settlement after the Great War that it endeavoured to give satisfaction to the national aspirations of the suppressed peoples of eastern and central Europe. The view is not commonly advanced that what has in the past been regarded as the principal merit of the settlement was in fact its fundamental defect, because the principle of national liberation "was utterly at variance with twentieth-century trends of political and economic organization."

It is not without profit to consider why the liberation of the suppressed nationalities of Europe came to be adopted as a principal war aim of the Allies. That peace would be best assured by redrawing the map of Europe along the lines of national division appeared a common-sense conclusion from the history of the last hundred years. Had not the primary cause of war throughout

From W. M. Jordan, *Great Britain, France and the German Problem 1918–1939* (London, 1943), pp. 218–225. Published on behalf of the Royal Institute of International Affairs. Reprinted by permission of Oxford University Press.

73

that period been the demand for national freedom in "the deadlands of Europe"? This line of reasoning, developed in almost every writing on war aims, was most succinctly expressed by Sir Herbert Samuel: "Unrest among a subject population, repression by the ruling power, sympathy and angry resentment in the neighbouring people nervous for their ascendancy, sterner repression as the result, and greater unrest again — this is the unhappy circle of events which, constantly recurring wherever national liberty is denied, maintains animosity and predisposes to war." Only in the speeches of President Wilson was the demand for national liberation given doctrinal form. To President Wilson the nation was a moral entity living within a community of nations the peace of which depended on equal respect for the rights of each member great and small; among these rights was numbered first and foremost the right to freedom from foreign rule. President Wilson spoke the language of moral obligation, whereas to the statesmen of the Entente the vague principle of national self-determination was rather a political maxim to be applied with due regard to time and circumstance. It may be added that the idea of national liberation could alone give meaning to the struggle which the Allies were waging from 1914 to 1918. Both in England and France it was admitted that a German triumph might bring peace and prosperity to the Continent — peace and prosperity to the Continent from the English Channel to the Dniester under a *Pax Germanica*. "There might be a Europe, there might be a rich and fairly peaceful Europe under Germany's domination: but the peace would be . . . an iron peace, and the riches would be produced for German masters by masses of men without freedom and almost without nationality." That small states would henceforward "only be able to maintain their independence with the utmost difficulty" was a peculiarly German doctrine; neither the interests nor the inclinations of Great Britain and France permitted its currency in the countries of the Entente. "Great

Britain is fighting," Asquith declared at the outset of the struggle, "to withstand, as we believe in the best interests not only of our own Empire but of civilization at large, the arrogant claim of a single Power to dominate the development of the destinies of Europe."

Comparatively little is known of any plans drawn up in 1914–1918 by the British and French Governments for the reorganization of Europe after the War. Probably there is little to know; the elaboration of detailed plans seemed futile until victory was assured. No memoranda are available to indicate the views of the French Government concerning the political settlement of Europe as a whole. For Great Britain all that is available are the papers drawn up in connection with the consideration of war aims and peace terms by the British Cabinet in October 1916, and by the Imperial War Cabinet in March 1917. But these are sufficient to show that to British statesmen the idea of re-drawing the map of Europe along the lines of national division commended itself the more because it would tend, so it seemed, to lessen the power of Germany in eastern and central Europe. A durable peace, Balfour advised in October 1916, can best be secured "by the double method of diminishing the area from which the Central Powers can draw the men and money required for a policy of aggression, while at the same time rendering a policy of aggression less attractive by rearranging the map of Europe in closer agreement with what we vaguely call the principle of nationality." The British Cabinet held the view — so General Smuts informed Count Mensdorff in December 1917 — that no peace could be satisfactory which left Germany in a position of military predominance on the Continent. "The political dispositions of Central Europe after the war," General Smuts added, "should afford some safeguard against the re-establishment." The territorial changes which the British Government had in mind were outlined by Balfour in a speech in the Imperial War Cabinet on 21st March 1917. Since the speech has not been published in any easily accessible work, it may be worth while quoting at length the relevant extract. "I frankly admit," Balfour declared, "that when the Germans say that we are fighting for a cause that means their destruction, it is not true in one sense: we are not destroying a German Germany, but we are trying to destroy the rather artificial creation of the modern Prussia, which includes many Slav elements which never belonged to Germany until about 140 years ago and ought, really, not to belong to Germany at this moment. . . ." Balfour welcomed the prospect of detaching from Germany her Polish provinces. "Personally," he added, "from a selfish Western point of view, I would rather that Poland was autonomous under the Russians, because if you make an absolutely independent Poland, lying between Russia and the Central States, you cut off Russia altogether from the West. Russia ceases to be a factor in Western politics, or almost ceases. She will be largely divided from Austria by Roumania. She will be divided from Germany by the new Polish State; and she will not be coterminous with any of the belligerents. And if Germany has designs in the future upon France or the West, I think she will be protected by this new State from any action on the part of Russia, and I am not at all sure that that is to the interests of Western civilization. It is a problem which has greatly exercised my mind, and for which I do not see a clear solution. These are disjointed observations in regard to Poland; they lead to no clear-cut recommendation on my part. I am not pleading for a cause; I am trying to lay before the Cabinet the various elements in the problem as they strike me." In Balfour's view, then, the interests of Europe would best be served if Poland, while enjoying a large measure of autonomy, were to remain an integral part of the Russian Empire, for only so would Russia remain a European Power so placed as to exercise direct pressure on Germany. But when the October Revolution had dispelled the possibility of such an arrangement, British and French thought moved toward complete independ-ence for Poland. Perhaps the most striking statement in Lloyd George's speech of 5th January 1918 was the declaration: "An independent Poland, comprising all those genuinely Polish elements who desire to form part of it, is an urgent necessity for the stability of Western Europe."

The application of the principle of national self-determination in the Danubian basin was the cause of more prolonged perplexity. In 1916 the Foreign Office looked forward without misgiving to the break-up of the Dual Monarchy and to the inclusion of German Austria in Germany. The Austrians, it was held, would swell the Catholic population within Germany and so create a counterpoise to Prussia. But Balfour was of a different mind, and his views came to prevail within the Cabinet. Fearing the fusion of the German-speaking population within a single powerful state, Balfour desired the maintenance of the Dual Monarchy. The British ideal for central Europe was an Empire liberalized by the grant of autonomy to the subject nationalities and redeemed from the domination of Prussia. This was the theme of Lloyd George's speech of 5th January 1918; this, too, was the sense of the tenth of the Fourteen Points. But Balfour in his speech to the Imperial War Cabinet in May 1917 had frankly confessed himself baffled by the obstacles to any such settlement. Transylvania had been promised to Roumania — that would break up historic Hungary; Bosnia and Herzegovina had been promised to Serbia, and Dalmatia to Italy — that might not break up the historic Austria; but the secession of Bohemia would do so — and the Czechs, Balfour admitted, had such a hatred of German civilization that they, too, would claim their freedom. As long as hope could be entertained of a separate peace with Austria, Allied statesmen refrained from any step likely to contribute to the entire collapse of the Hapsburg Empire. But before the cessation of hostilities the foundations of the Czechoslovak state had been laid by the recognition of the Czecho-slovaks as an allied and belligerent nation.

The controversy between Lloyd George and Clemenceau at the Peace Conference regarding the eastern frontiers of Germany is well known. "I would therefore take as a guiding principle of the peace," declared Lloyd George in his Memorandum of 26th March, "that as far as is humanly possible the different races should be allocated to their motherlands, and that this human criterion should have precedence over considerations of strategy or economics or communications, which can usually be adjusted by other means." Clemenceau's reply, five days later, was indicative of his determination to endeavour to strengthen Poland and Czechoslovakia as barriers against the expansion of German power in eastern and central Europe. "Our firmest guarantee against German aggression," he remarked in the Council of Four, "is that behind Germany, in an excellent strategic position, stand Czechoslovakia and Poland." But this controversy between the British and French premiers at the end of March conveys a somewhat distorted impression of the relations of the British and French delegations on frontier questions. Neither the question of the Czech-German frontier, nor indeed even the problem of Austria, provoked any conflict of opinion between the British and the French. The inclusion within Czechoslovakia of the German-inhabited territories of Bohemia was never in doubt. Even before the Peace Conference opened, Dr. Beneš is said to have obtained from the three European Great Powers — from France on 28th September 1918, and from Great Britain and Italy on 7th January 1919 — pledges of support for the Czech claims to these borderlands. All the members of the Commission on Czechoslovak claims, British, French, Italian, and American alike, agreed in recommending that the historic frontier of Bohemia should in principle be adopted as the frontier of the new state. The considerations which they advanced in support of their recommendation are not without interest:

(a) *Economic reasons*. The whole of the region occupied by the Germans of Bohemia is industrially and commercially dependent upon Bohemia rather than upon Germany. The Germans of Bohemia cannot exist without the economic co-operation of the Czechs, nor the Czechs without the economic co-operation of the Germans. There is between them a complete interdependence in this respect. . . .

(d) *Reasons of national security*. These reasons depend on geographic considerations. The chain of mountains which surrounds Bohemia constitutes a line of defense for the country. To take away this line of mountains would be to place Bohemia at the mercy of the Germans.

On the question of German Austria there appears also to have been remarkably little difference of opinion, and still less discussion, at the Peace Conference. Until March the question of Austria attracted curiously little attention. Though in December 1918 Pichon had declared in the Chamber his determination to prevent the inclusion of the Austrian Germans within Germany, no action was taken until, on 4th March 1919, the Austrian Constituent Assembly proceeded to accept as part of the organic law of Austria the resolution: "German Austria is a constituent part of the German Reich." At this stage the French Government intervened. On 11th March Tardieu notified his colleagues Philip Kerr and Dr. Mezes of the French desire to require from Germany an undertaking to recognize the independence of German Austria, and to undertake to do nothing, either of a political or of an economic nature, which directly or indirectly could violate this independence. Kerr replied mildly that he had no instructions; he thought that such a provision might be accepted as a temporary measure pending the settlement of Austria-Hungary and the setting up of the League of Nations. Clemenceau, however, waited till the end of April before submitting to the Council of Four the resolution which was the origin of Article 88 of the Treaty of Versailles: "Germany acknowledges and will fully respect the independence of Austria. . . ." Of the discussion preceding the adoption of

Clemenceau's resolution no record has been published.

In the fixing of the German frontiers in eastern and central Europe only the question of the Polish-German frontier gave rise to acute Franco-British controversy. The divergent attitudes of France and Great Britain first became evident during the preparation of armistice terms. In the Supreme War Council on 2nd November 1918 Pichon proposed that the Germans should be required to evacuate all the territories which had formed part of the Kingdom of Poland before 1772. Balfour replied that the Allies were committed only "to reconstitute a Poland composed of Poles"; the 1772 frontier, he added, would involve not only the inclusion of territory not inhabited by Poles, but the exclusion of Polish-inhabited territory. French insistence on the frontiers of 1772 thereafter ceased; Cambon's note of 26th November 1918, which outlined the French demands, required no more than a strict application of Balfour's principle. But Point X of the Fourteen Points involved a further complication. "An independent Polish state should be erected which should include the territories inhabited and secure access to the sea. . . ." Free and secure access to the sea? It was the unanimous view of the experts of the Polish Commission — British, French, Italian, and American — that "free and secure access to the sea" could be assured to Poland only by incorporating within Poland not only the German-inhabited town of Danzig, but also the German-inhabited Kreis of Marienwerder, which was traversed by the Danzig-Mlawa-Warsaw railway. Challenged on this point by Lloyd George, and invited by the Council of Ten to reconsider its recommendations, the Commission reaffirmed its view. Lloyd George nevertheless prevailed on Wilson and Clemenceau to agree to the establishment of a special régime in Danzig, and to a plebiscite to determine the fate of Marienwerder, which in the outcome remained German. As regards Danzig, the writer of the authoritative study on *The Peace Settlement in the German-Polish Borderlands** has recorded his conclusion that the vagueness of the hastily drafted Danzig clauses of the Treaty of Versailles may in the ultimate analysis be found the origin of the recurring Polish disputes.

With the outcome of Lloyd George's efforts with regard to Danzig it is of interest to compare the settlement eventually reached with regard to Upper Silesia. In response to German protests, Lloyd George insisted on a plebiscite also in this area, which according to the initial conditions of peace was to have been ceded outright to Poland. The voting on 20th March 1921 — 60 per cent for Germany, 40 per cent for Poland — precipitated a prolonged Anglo-French dispute. In the industrial area the communes which had voted for Poland were inextricably intermixed with those which had voted for Germany. Ought the industrial area to be divided between the two countries? Neither Great Britain nor France inclined to this view: but whereas France desired the transfer of the area to Poland, Great Britain insisted on its retention by Germany. Neither country took its stand by a strict interpretation of the plebiscite. On 12th August the Supreme Council escaped the deadlock by inviting the Council of the League to recommend the line of the frontier between Poland and Germany. Two months later the League Council made its recommendations. A frontier was proposed which cut through the industrial area in order to conform as precisely as possible with the wishes of the inhabitants expressed in the plebiscite, while a general convention was to be concluded between Poland and Germany to safeguard the continuity of economic activity. The upper Silesian Convention, both in its negotiation and subsequent operation, is justly regarded as a model international experiment.

* Ian F. D. Morrow. See *Suggestions for Additional Reading*. [EDITOR'S NOTE]

THE WORLD CRISIS: THE TERRITORIAL
SETTLEMENTS OF 1919-1920

WINSTON S. CHURCHILL

By 1919 Winston Churchill's career already included extensive experience as a soldier, writer, Home Secretary, and First Lord of the Admiralty. Simultaneously with the opening of the peace conference he became Secretary of State for War and Air. In 1923 he embarked on a multi-volume study of the World War which, by 1929, resulted in the publication of the fourth and last volume of the series, dealing with the peace settlement, from which the following selection is drawn. In it, Churchill assesses the soundness of the territorial changes wrought on the map of Europe.

However keen may be the feelings excited by the distribution of tropical colonies, of compensation in money or in kind and of retributive justice; high as are the hopes centered in the League of Nations, it is by the territorial settlements in Europe that the Treaties of 1919 and 1920 will finally be judged. Here we are in contact with those deep and lasting facts which cast races of men into moulds and fix their place and status in the world. Here we stir the embers of the past and light the beacons of the future. Old flags are raised anew; the passions of vanished generations awake; beneath the shell-torn soil of the twentieth century the bones of the long dead warriors and victims are exposed, and the wail of the lost causes sounds in the wind.

The treaties with which we now have to deal take their place in the great series which includes the Treaty of Westphalia, the Treaty of Utrecht and the Treaties of Vienna. They are at once the latest and the largest link in the chain of European history. They will be memorable for three events of the first magnitude: the dissolution of the Austro-Hungarian Empire; the rebirth of Poland; and the preservation of united Germany. Even the short distance we have travelled since the Conference in Paris reveals the scale of these monarch-peaks, and how they tower above the range and dominate the wide regions of mountainous and hilly country. Already through the clearer air we can discern the proportions of the vast landscape and its massive simplicity. The Empire of Charles V, and with it the Hapsburg Monarchy, the survivor of so many upheavals, the main structure of central and southern Europe, is represented only by a chasm. The three sundered parts of Poland are re-united into a sovereign independent Republic of thirty million souls; and Germany, beaten and disarmed upon the field of battle, defenceless before her outraged conquerors, rises the largest and incomparably the strongest racial mass in Europe.

These dominant facts in the life of Europe did not spring solely, or even mainly, from the volcanic violence of the war. They were the result of the methodical application of a principle. If the treaty makers of

From Winston S. Churchill, *The World Crisis, The Aftermath* (London, 1929), pp. 202–206, 214–216, 222–231. Reprinted by permission of Odhams Press Ltd.

Vienna in 1814 were ruled by the principle of Legitimacy, those in Paris in 1919 were guided by the principle of Self-determination. Although the expression "Self-determination" will rightly be forever connected with the name of President Wilson, the ideal was neither original nor new. The phrase itself is Fichte's *"Selbst bestimmung."* The conception has never been more forcefully presented than by Mazzini. Throughout the British Empire it had long been known and widely practiced under somewhat less explosive precepts of "Self-Government" and "Government by Consent." During the nineteenth century the rise of Nationalism made it increasingly plain that all great Empires must reckon with this principle and increasingly conform to it, if they were to survive united and vital in the modern world. The almost complete exclusion of religion in all its forms from the political sphere had left Nationalism the most powerful moulding instrument of mankind in temporal affairs.

The Fourteen Points embodied and proclaimed the principle of Self-determination. In his speeches the President had declared that "national aspirations must be respected. Peoples may now be dominated and governed only by their own consent. Self-determination is not a mere phrase." "Peoples and provinces are not to be bartered about from sovereignty to sovereignty. . . . Every territorial settlement must be made in the interest and for the benefit of the populations concerned. . . . All well-defined and national aspirations shall be accorded the utmost satisfaction that can be accorded them without introducing new or perpetuating old elements of discord and antagonism." The Allies had earnestly identified their war aims with this declaration. The Germans had accompanied their requests for an armistice by the conditions that the peace settlement should be based upon the Fourteen Points of President Wilson and his other speeches. They had even claimed that they laid down their arms and rendered themselves defenceless upon this understanding. Therefore the principle of Self-determination was at once what the victors had fought for and the vanquished claimed.

Here was one clear guiding principle upon which all the peoples so cruelly sundered, so torn with wounds and hatreds, were united, and to which all were bound both by faith and interest. The main and imperative duty of the Peace Conference, in all matters comprised in their task of making peace between the belligerents, was to give effect to this principle; or in words which I venture to requote, "to liberate the captive nationalities, to reunite those branches of the same family which had long been arbitrarily divided, and to draw frontiers in broad accordance with the ethnic masses."

All being agreed upon the fundamental principle, it remained to apply it. But if the principle was simple and accepted, its application was difficult and disputable. What was to be the test of nationality? How were the wishes of "national elements" to be expressed and obtained? How and where were the resulting frontiers to be drawn amid entangled populations? To what extent should the main principle override every other consideration — historical, geographical, economic, or strategic? How far could the armed and vehement forces which were everywhere afoot be brought to accept the resulting decisions? Such were the problems of the Peace Conference, and in particular of the Triumvirate.

In the main it was decided that language should be adopted as the proof of nationality. No doubt language is not always its manifestation. Some of the most nationally conscious stocks can scarcely speak their own language at all, or only with the greatest difficulty. Some oppressed races spoke the language of their oppressors, while hating them; and some dominant breeds spoke the language of their subjects, while ruling them. Still matters had to be settled with reasonable dispatch, and no better guide to the principle of nationality in disputed cases could be found than language; or, as a last resort, a plebiscite.

It was inherent in the realities that the

scheme of drawing frontiers in accordance with nationality as defined by language or with the wish of the local inhabitants could not in practice be applied without modification. Some of the new States had no access to the sea through their own populations, and could not become effective economic units without such access. Some liberated nationalities had for centuries looked forward to regaining the ancient frontiers of their long vanished sovereignty. Some of the victors were entitled by treaty to claim, and others of the victors bound by treaty to accord them, frontiers fixed not by language or the wish of the inhabitants, but by Alps. Some integral economic communities lay athwart the ethnic frontier; and at many points rival and hostile races were intermingled, not only as individuals but by villages, by townships and by rural districts. All this debatable ground had to be studied and fought over mile by mile by the numerous, powerful, and violently agitated States concerned.

Nevertheless all these reservations and impingements upon the fundamental principle affected only the outskirts of peoples and countries. All the disputable areas put together were but a minute fraction of Europe. They were but exceptions which proved the rule. Fierce as were and are the irritations which have arisen wherever these sensitive and doubtful fringes of nationality have been roughly clipped by frontier scissors, they do not impair the broad essence of the treaties. Probably less than 3 per cent of the European population are now living under Governments whose nationality they repudiate; and the map of Europe has for the first time been drawn in general harmony with the wishes of its peoples.

* * *

Judged by Gladstonian standards, Germany issued from the war and the peace with many positive advantages. She had in fact realized all the main objectives of British Liberal policy in the Victorian era. Defeat has given the German people effective control of their own affairs. The Impe-rialist system has been swept away. A domestic self-determination has been achieved. A parliamentary system based on universal suffrage to which the rulers of Germany are effectively responsible may be some consolation for the loss of twenty two kings and princes. The abolition of compulsory military service has always seemed to British eyes a boon and not an injury. The restriction of armaments enforced by treaties upon Germany is today extolled as the highest goal to which all nations should aspire. The absurd and monstrous economic and financial chapters of the Treaty of Versailles have already been swept almost entirely into limbo; they have either lapsed or have been superseded by a series of arrangements increasingly based on facts, on good sense, and on mutual agreement. The sufferings of the German bourgeois and rentier classes, the humble pensioner, the thrifty annuitant, the retired toiler, the aged professor, the brave officer — which resulted from the act of repudiation involved in the destruction of the mark largely by the German Government themselves — are piteous. They may affront the justice of the German State; they have not weakened the pulsations of the German heart, nor the productive vitality of German industry, nor even the credit and saving power of the German people. Germany has lost her colonies, but she was a late-comer on the colonial scene. She possessed no territory over-seas in which the German race could live and multiply. "Foreign plantations," to quote the old-fashioned English phrase, in tropical lands might be a source of pride and interest and certainly of expenditure. They were in any case hostages to a stronger sea-power. Their alienation in no way impaired the German strength and very doubtfully improved the fortunes of their new possessors.

Contrast for a moment the position which Germany occupies today with the doom which would have fallen upon the British Empire and upon Great Britain itself had the submarine attack mastered the Royal Navy and left our forty millions only the choice between unconditional surrender and certain starvation. Half the severity meted out by the Treaty of Versailles would have involved not only the financial ruin of our ancient, slowly built-up world organization but a swift contraction of the British population by at least ten million souls and the condemnation of the rest to universal and hopeless poverty. The stakes of this hideous war were beyond all human measure, and for Britain and her people they were not less than final extinction. When we consider the fate of the Austro-Hungarian Empire, of Austria itself, and of the overcrowded city of Vienna, we may measure in miniature the risks we were forced to run.

In these blunt paragraphs there is an appeal to the intellect of Germany.

*   *   *

The fierce stresses of the settlement of the German peace terms had exhausted for the time being the energies of the Triumvirate. It was natural that they should shrink from immediately plunging into the less critical but none the less important and even more complicated problems of the Austro-Hungarian Empire and its fate. Some lassitude was inevitable and perhaps excusable. Numerous Commissions had long been working upon the various aspects. It seemed sufficient at the moment to give a general direction to these Commissions and to the drafting Committee of jurists to apply the principles of the treaty with Germany in framing the treaties with the other defeated States.

But the principle of Self-determination which had preserved Germany as the greatest united branch of the European family was finally fatal to the Empire of the Hapsburgs. Moreover, in this vast scene the decisive events had already taken place. The Austro-Hungarian Empire had in fact shivered into fragments in the last fortnight of the war. On October 28, 1918, Czechoslovakia had proclaimed itself and had been recognized by the Allied and Associated Powers as an independent sovereign state. Strong in the memories of the Czechoslovak

army corps and in the influence upon the Allies of Masaryk and Beneš, the Czechoslovaks successfully presented themselves at the Peace Conference, not as a part of an enemy empire defeated by the Allies, but as a new state technically at war with Germany and Austria and awaiting peace settlements with both these countries. A similar metamorphosis had accompanied the creation on December 1, 1918, of Jugo-Slavia, formed from the union of the victorious Serbians and the defeated Croats and the Slovenes into a Southern Slav Kingdom of approximately 13,000,000 souls. This new State was also promptly recognized by Great Britain, France, and the United States; Italy, however, demurred. The Croats, they complained, were enemies who had fought hard and well against Italy throughout the war. Whatever might be said of Bohemia and the Czechoslovaks, the Croats had no right to change sides in the moment of defeat and by a judicious dive emerge among the victors. However the force of events prevailed. The Croats sought, and the Serbians accorded shelter and status as a friendly people forced into war against their will by a defunct and guilty Imperialism. Their claims were recognized by Italy in April 1919.

Hungary had also seceded from the Empire and proclaimed herself an independent monarchy. Austria isolated with the ancient and cultured capital of Vienna in her midst endeavoured to tread a similar path. The Austrians proclaimed a Republic, declared that they were a new State which had never been at war with the Allies and pleaded that its people ought not to be penalized for the misdeeds of a vanished régime.

These transformations confronted the reunited Council of Four with novel problems. The representatives of Czechoslovakia and Jugo-Slavia were ensconced as friends and in part as allies within the charmed circle of victory. The Austrians and the Hungarians who had fought at their side on the same fronts and in the same armies sat outside under the shadow of defeat and the stigma of war-guilt. Although the ruling class in Austria and Hungary bore an exceptional responsibility, it was absurd to regard the mass of the populations of any of these four States as peculiarly innocent or culpable. All had been drawn by the same currents irresistibly into the vortex. Yet one half were to be cherished and the other half to be smitten.

Two soldiers have served side by side, sharing in a common cause the perils and hardships of the war. The war is ended and they return to their respective villages. But a frontier line has been drawn between them. One is a guilty wretch lucky to escape with life the conquerors' vengeance. The other appears to be one of the conquerors himself. Alas for these puppets of Fate! It is always unlucky to be born in the central regions of any continent.

It was to this strange and tumultuous scene that the Peace Conference endeavoured to apply the principle of Self-determination which had governed the German Treaty, and thus redraw the map of Central Europe. The word "Czechoslovakia" was new to British ears; but the ancient kingdom of Bohemia and Moravia, where the Czechs lived, stirred popular memories of King Wenceslas on the Feast of Stephen, of blind King John of Bohemia at the Battle of Crécy, of the Prince of Wales's Feathers with its German motto "Ich Dien," and perhaps of John Huss of Prague. Here were time-honoured tales. For several hundred years we had lost sight of Bohemia. The personal union of the Crowns of Austria and Bohemia, effected in the sixteenth century, had made the head of the Hapsburgs Austrian Emperor and King of Bohemia. The torment of the Thirty Years War scarred for ever the history of the two countries. Bohemia, persecuted for Protestantism, became partly Catholicized under duress. From 1618, after the total defeat of the Bohemians in the Battle of the White Mountain, the Hapsburgs ruled a conquered kingdom with autocratic power. The Bohemian people were never reconciled. Their national sentiment slumbered during the eighteenth century; but memories were long and tradition powerful. The latter half of the nineteenth century saw the rebirth of Bohemian nationalism embodied in the Czech movement. Popular education revived here as elsewhere a long-forgotten national language. The schools became the centres of strife between the Czech population and the Imperial Government. Lingual self-consciousness and national aspirations rose together. The Emperor Francis Joseph had been crowned King of Hungary at Budapest; but the Czech desire that he should come to Prague and be crowned King of Bohemia was obstinately and, as it now seems, insensately, refused.

During the war the Czech movement developed into the demand for autonomy and thence into independence. The Czechs had been accustomed to look to Russia for sympathy. After the Russian Revolution they turned under the guidance of Masaryk to the United States and to the Western Powers. Their independence had already been recognized. It remained to define their frontiers. But here were stubborn complications. Bohemia and Moravia contained at least three millions of German-speaking population, often concentrated, usually in the ascendant, a strong, competent stock holding firmly together like the Ulstermen in Ireland. To exclude the German-speaking population was deeply and perhaps fatally to weaken the new State; to include them was to affront the principle of Self-determination. The Peace Conference in this dilemma decided to adhere to the ancient frontiers of Bohemia, well defined by mountain ranges, and consecrated by five hundred years of tradition. Apart from some vexatious but petty alterations on the frontier towards Austria, this decision became effective.

The Czechs of Bohemia had joined hands with the Slovaks. This tribe dwelt upon the southern slopes of the mountains on the north of Hungary, and stretched some distance into the Danubian plain. The Slovaks had for centuries been under Magyar rule which they regarded as oppressive. They were a Slav people akin to the Czechs. They spoke a dialect of the same language. They wished to escape from Hungary and join the new State. President Wilson toward the close of the war had agreed with Professor Masaryk that the United States would support the inclusion of the Slovaks in the new Bohemia; and on this Czechoslovakia had, as we have seen, proclaimed itself a sovereign State. The drawing of the frontier between the Slovaks and the Magyars was in any case a task of difficulty. No line could be drawn to which there were not valid objections. The natural bias of the Commission was in favor of the Slovaks, and as a result about a million Magyars found themselves included against their will within the limits of Czechoslovakia.

The Kingdom of Jugo-Slavia had formed itself by the union of the old Kingdom of Serbia, augmented by the Provinces of Bosnia and Herzegovina, with the Croats and the Slovenes. The Croats had for centuries been under the Hungarian crown. They were not down-trodden like the Slovaks, but a home rule movement was in progress among them by constitutional and legal methods before the war. The Dalmatians and the Slovenes, who inhabited the mountainous country north and north-west of Venice and Trieste, were subject to the Austrian crown. Both these populations sought a new allegiance and the new Serb-Croat-Slovene Kingdom, denoted by the initials S. H. S. entered upon the troubles of existence.

Again the limits of the new State had to be determined. The frontiers of Jugo-Slavia with Hungary presented little difficulty; with Austria they were more difficult, and at least one plebiscite was required to mitigate the sharpness of decisions. The frontiers with Italy were the most difficult of all; and here victorious Allied Governments faced each other in armed menace. The Italian frontiers of Jugo-Slavia were eventually settled by separate negotiations between the two countries.

Roumania, like Serbia, was to gain a great accession of population and territory. The crescent moon of the Roumanian map waxed to full by the incorporation of Transylvania. The problem of Transylvania was insoluble by the principle of Self-determination. It presented the feature of a considerable Hungarian population isolated within a Roumanian border belt. The peoples of the Roumanian zone wished to join Roumania; those of the Magyar nucleus to adhere to their kinsmen in Hungary. Either decision would have conflicted with Self-determination. The issues of principle being thus physically excluded and the integrity of Transylvania being an important factor, the Peace Conference transferred the whole country to Roumania and thus alienated at least another million Magyars from Hungary.

The new limits of Hungary and Austria were the result of these events. Hungary lost Slovakia to Bohemia, Croatia to Serbia, Transylvania to Roumania. She was also required to cede to Austria a considerable German speaking area near Vienna which was essential to the food supplies of that forlorn capital. It happened unluckily for the Magyars that they had lost command of their own government in the critical period of the Paris Conference. A Communist revolution had erupted in Budapest. Bela Kun, a disciple of Lenin and a paid tool of Moscow, had seized power and had used it with cruel violence and tyranny. The Supreme Council could only expostulate. It therefore expostulated. But the Roumanian Army was in Transylvania. Attacked by communist rabble this army advanced as invaders of Hungary and were at first welcomed in the guise of deliverers by the Hungarian population whom they mercilessly pillaged. The Hungarian people were therefore at their weakest when the crucial issues of their future were to be decided. Not only were the various subject races, which Hungary had in the course of centuries incorporated, liberated from her sway, but more than two and a half million Magyars, a fourth of the entire population, dwell today under foreign rule.

Austria is the final remnant. With Hungary she bore the whole blame and burden of the once mighty Hapsburg Empire. Reduced to a community of six millions around Vienna and in the Alpine Lands, with the Imperial Capital of two millions in its midst, the state of Austria was pitiful indeed. The frontier had still to be drawn between Austria and Italy. The secret Treaty of London had promised Italy the line of the Alps. Italy claimed her Treaty rights, and England and France were bound. President Wilson was free, and his problem was painful. On the one hand stood the principle of Self-determination; on the other, the Alps, the Treaties and the strategic security of Italy. In April President Wilson withdrew the opposition he had hitherto maintained and the Southern Tyrol passed to Italian sovereignty.

It should be added that in all the treaties constituting the frontiers of the new States precise and elaborate provisions were inserted and accepted providing for the protection of minorities, their good treatment and equal rights before the law. Italy as one of the victorious Great Powers was not called upon to assume a treaty obligation for the protection of minorities. She instead voluntarily declared her solemn resolve to accord them the consideration and fair play which were their due. The inhabitants of the South Tyrol may therefore base themselves directly and in a peculiarly personal sense upon the faith and honour of the Italian nation.

In her miserable plight Austria turned to Germany. A union with the great Teutonic mass would give to Austria vitality and means of existence from which she was cut off by a circle of resentful neighbours. The new Austrian Government appealing at once to the right of Self-determination and of nationality, claimed to become a part of the German Republic. Theoretically upon Wilsonian principles this demand — the Anschluss, as it is called — was difficult to resist. In practice it was loaded with danger. It would have meant making the new Germany larger in territory and population than the old Germany which had

already proved strong enough to fight the world for four years. It would have brought the frontiers of the German realm to the summits of the Alps and made a complete barrier between Eastern and Western Europe. The future of Switzerland and the permanent existence of Czechoslovakia alike appeared to be affected. A clause was therefore inserted both in the German and Austrian Treaties forbidding such union except with the unanimous consent, presumably unattainable, of the Council of the League of Nations.

The exclusion of this alternative for the gravest reasons of European peace made it the more necessary to improve the conditions in the new Austria. This required a speedy recognition of the Republic, and the greatest care to lighten the financial burden imposed upon it. Notwithstanding the urgent representations made by those Englishmen who were actually in Vienna, the whole Austrian question was for months completely neglected. When at last the drafting of the Austrian Treaty began, the different Commissions endeavored to apply to it the terms of the German Treaty. This meant that the whole financial burden was to be laid on the small Austrian Republic, together with Hungary. The Reparation clauses technically imposed the onus of paying reparations for the whole of the former Austro-Hungarian Monarchy upon these two small derelict States. This pure nonsense could of course never be applied. But a needless and dangerous delay arose. The complete financial collapse of Austria followed, and a social collapse was only averted at a later stage by the intervention of the League of Nations at the insistence chiefly of Mr. Balfour.

Bulgaria was better treated; she missed the hiatus and inertia which followed the Treaty of Versailles. She profited by the recoil from the decisions of the Treaty of St. Germain. Her population was scarcely at all reduced; her economic and geographical needs were studied; she was assured of commercial access to the Aegean. Yet the griefs of the Allies against the Bulgarians were not light. The cold-blooded entry of Bulgaria into the war; the historic ingratitude which this act involved to Russian liberators and English friends; the stabbing of struggling Serbia in the back; the frightful injury inflicted thereby upon the Allied Cause; the war crimes committed on Serbian soil — all these made a long and dark account. Dr. Temperley states in his History of the Peace Conference that the Bulgarian delegation was surprised on their arrival at Paris by the fact that no one wished to shake hands with them, and a pregnant footnote sets forth many gruesome explanations of this coolness. Yet the Bulgarian Treaty was drafted in a far more instructed and careful mood than that which had regulated the fate of Austria and Hungary. The experts were becoming adepts in the work of treaty making; the best and ablest officials were acquiring control. The passions and interest of the Great Powers were not involved; they were indeed benevolently indifferent. The worst complaint of the Bulgarians was that they were forbidden to have a conscript army and that their people would not become professional soldiers. For the rest they were a warrior race, industrious and brave, apt to till and defend their soil or take the soil of others. They sat on the ground-floor of life's edifice, with no great risk of falling further. It was accepted they had been driven into the war by King Ferdinand, and with his departure into luxurious exile the wrath of the Allies had been sensibly appeased.

It is with the general aspects of the territorial settlements with the Central Powers, and the principles underlying them, that this chapter is mainly concerned. . . . It is obvious how many points of friction remained to cause heart-burnings to the populations affected, and anxiety to Europe. But a fair judgment upon settlement, a simple explanation of how it arose, cannot leave the authors of the new map of Europe under serious reproach. To an overwhelming extent the wishes of the various populations prevailed. The fundamental principle which governed the victors was honestly applied within the limits of their waning power. No solution could have been free from hardship and anomaly. More refined solutions in the disputed areas could only have been obtained if Britain, France, and the United States had been prepared to provide considerable numbers of troops for lengthy periods to secure a far more elaborate and general adoption of plebiscites, to effect transferences of population such as were afterwards made in Turkey, and meanwhile to supply food and credits to those whose destinies would thus be held in suspense. The exhaustion of the war forbade such toilsome interferences, nor would the scale of the remaining grievances have justified their hazards. The moulds into which Central and Southern Europe has been cast were hastily and in parts roughly shaped, but they conformed for all practical purposes with much exactness to the general design; and according to the lights of the twentieth century that design seems true.

THE *DIKTAT* OF VERSAILLES

ADOLF HITLER

Hitler's obsession with the evils of "Versailles," in addition to Jews, Masons, and Marxists, furnished the leitmotif for the Nazi propaganda onslaught in the 1920's and 1930's. Son of a petty official in the Habsburg civil service, Hitler spent a shiftless and lonely youth, moving about Vienna and Munich, until the outbreak of war in 1914 brought him personal relief from purposeless existence. Already passionate in his admiration of the glory of German history, he joined the German army in which he rose to the rank of corporal. The defeat of Imperial Germany, however, which caught him convalescing in a hospital near Berlin from wounds suffered on the Somme in 1916, created for him an emotional crisis of prime magnitude. In it he found his mission: to lead Germany back upon the path of glory. Using the Treaty of Versailles after 1919 as an explanation for all German woes, he gained a popular platform and a convenient slogan, easily distorted to suit the purposes of the Nazi movement. Hitler's cynical manipulation of the Versailles *issue* and his interesting rejection of Germany's 1914 frontiers as a basis for future treaty revision are elaborated in the following passages, reprinted from *Mein Kampf*.

WHEN in the year 1919 the German people was burdened with the peace treaty, we should have been justified in hoping that precisely through this instrument of boundless repression the cry for German freedom would have been immensely promoted. *Peace treaties whose demands are a scourge to nations not seldom strike the first roll of drums for the uprising to come.*

What could have been done with this peace treaty of Versailles?!

This instrument of boundless extortion and abject humiliation might, in the hands of a willing government, have become an instrument for whipping up the national passions to fever heat. With a brilliant propagandist exploitation of these sadistic cruelties, the indifference of a people might have been raised to indignation, and indignation to blazing fury!

How could every single one of these points have been burned into the brain and emotion of this people, until finally in sixty million heads, in men and women, a common sense of shame and a common hatred would have become a single fiery sea of flame, from whose heat a will as hard as steel would have risen and a cry burst forth:

Give us arms again!

Yes, my friends, that is what such a peace treaty would do. In the boundlessness of its oppression, the shamelessness of its demands, lies the greatest propaganda weapon for the reawakening of a nation's dormant spirits of life.

For this, to be sure, from the child's primer down to the last newspaper, every theater and every movie house, every advertising pillar and every billboard, must be pressed into the service of this one great mission, until the timorous prayer of our

From Adolph Hitler, *Mein Kampf* (Boston, 1943). Translated by Ralph Manheim, pp. 632–633, 463–464, 649–654. Reprinted by permission of Houghton Mifflin Company.

present parlor patriots: "Lord, make us free!" is transformed in the brain of the smallest boy into the burning plea: *"Almighty God, bless our arms when the time comes; be just as thou hast always been; judge now whether we be deserving of freedom; Lord, bless our battle!"*

All this was neglected and nothing was done.

Who, then, will be surprised that our people is not as it should be and could be? If the rest of the world sees in us only a stooge, an obsequious dog, who gratefully licks the hands that have just beaten him?

Certainly our capacity for alliances today is injured by our people, but most of all by its governments. They in their corruption are to blame if after eight years of the most unlimited oppression so little will for freedom is present.

Much, therefore, as an active alliance policy is linked with the necessary evaluation of our people, the latter is equally dependent on the existence of a governmental power which does not want to be a handyman for foreign countries, not a taskmaster over its own strength, but a herald of the national conscience.

If our people has a state leadership which sees its mission in this light, six years will not pass before a bold Reich leadership in the field of foreign affairs will dispose of an equally bold will on the part of a people thirsting for freedom.

*   *   *

The first great meeting on February 24, 1920, in the Festsaal [Banquet Hall] of the Hofbräuhaus, had not died down in our ears when the preparations for the next were made. While up till then it had been considered risky to hold a little meeting once a month or even once every two weeks in a city like Munich, a large mass meeting was now to take place every seven days; in other words, once a week. I do not need to assure you that there was but one fear that constantly tormented us: would the people come and would they listen to us? — though I personally, even then, had the

unshakable conviction that once they were there, the people would stay and follow the speech.

In this period the Festsaal of the Munich Hofbräuhaus assumed an almost sacred significance for us National Socialists. Every week a meeting, almost always in this room, and each time the hall better filled and the people more devoted. Beginning with the "War Guilt," which at that time nobody bothered about, and the "Peace Treaties," nearly everything was taken up that seemed agitationally expedient or ideologically necessary. Especially to the peace treaties themselves the greatest attention was given. What prophecies the young movement kept making to the great masses! And nearly all of which have now been realized! Today it is easy to speak or write about these things. But in those days a public mass meeting, attended, not by bourgeois shopkeepers, but by incited proletarians, and dealing with the topic, "The Peace Treaty of Versailles," was taken as an attack on the Republic and a sign of a reactionary if not monarchistic attitude. At the very first sentence containing a criticism of Versailles, you had the stereotyped cry flung at you: "What about Brest-Litovsk?" "And Brest-Litovsk?" The masses roared this again and again, until gradually they grew hoarse or the speaker finally gave up his attempt to convince them. You felt like dashing your head against the wall in despair over such people! They did not want to hear or understand that Versailles was a shame and a disgrace, and not even that this dictated peace was an unprecedented pillaging of our people. The destructive work of the Marxists and the poison of enemy propaganda had deprived the people of any sense. And yet we had not even the right to complain! For how immeasurably great was the blame on another side! What had the bourgeoisie done to put a halt to this frightful disintegration, to oppose it and open the way to truth by a better and more thorough enlightenment? Nothing, and again nothing. In those days I saw them nowhere, all the great folkish apostles of today. Perhaps they spoke in little clubs, at teatables, or in circles of like-minded people, but where they should have been, among the wolves, they did not venture; except if there was a chance to howl with the pack.

But to me it was clear in those days that for the small basic nucleus which for the present constituted the movement, the question of war guilt had to be cleared up, and cleared up in the sense of historic truth. That our movement should transmit to the broadest masses knowledge of the peace treaty was the premise for the future success of the movement. At that time, when they all still regarded this peace as a success of democracy, we had to form a front against it and engrave ourselves forever in the minds of men as an enemy of this treaty, so that later, when the harsh reality of this treacherous frippery would be revealed in its naked hate, the recollection of our position at that time would win us confidence.

*   *   *

I still wish briefly to take a position on the question as to what extent the demand for soil and territory seems ethically and morally justified. This is necessary, since unfortunately, even in so-called folkish circles, all sorts of unctuous big-mouths step forward, endeavoring to set the rectification of the injustice of 1918 as the aim of the German nation's endeavors in the field of foreign affairs, but at the same time find it necessary to assure the whole world of folkish brotherhood and sympathy.

I should like to make the following preliminary remarks: *The demand for restoration of the frontiers of 1914 is a political absurdity of such proportions and consequences as to make it seem a crime. Quite aside from the fact that the Reich's frontiers in 1914 were anything but logical. For in reality they were neither complete in the sense of embracing the people of German nationality, nor sensible with regard to geomilitary expediency. They were not the result of a considered political action, but momentary frontiers in a political struggle that was by no means concluded; partly, in*

fact, they were the results of chance. With equal right and in many cases with more right, some other sample year of German history could be picked out, and the restoration of the conditions at that time declared to be the aim of an activity in foreign affairs. The above demand is entirely suited to our bourgeois society, which here as elsewhere does not possess a single creative political idea for the future, but lives only in the past, in fact, in the most immediate past; for even their backward gaze does not extend beyond their own times. The law of inertia binds them to a given situation and causes them to resist any change in it, but without ever increasing the activity of this opposition beyond the mere power of perseverance. So it is obvious that the political horizon of these people does not extend beyond the year 1914. By proclaiming the restoration of those borders as the political aim of their activity, they keep mending the crumbling league of our adversaries. Only in this way can it be explained that eight years after a world struggle in which states, some of which had the most heterogeneous desires, took part, the coalition of the victors of those days can still maintain itself in a more or less unbroken form.

All these states were at one time beneficiaries of the German collapse. Fear of our strength caused the greed and envy of the individual great powers among themselves to recede. By grabbing as much of the Reich as they could, they found the best guard against a future uprising. A bad conscience and fear of our people's strength is still the most enduring cement to hold together the various members of this alliance.

And we do not disappoint them. By setting up the restoration of the borders of 1914 as a political program for Germany, our bourgeoisie frighten away every partner who might desire to leave the league of our enemies, since he must inevitably fear to be attacked singly and thereby lose the protection of his individual fellow allies. Each single state feels concerned and threatened by this slogan.

Moreover, it is senseless in two respects:

(1) because the instruments of power are lacking to remove it from the vapors of club evenings into reality; and

(2) because, if it could actually be realized, the outcome would again be so pitiful that, by God, it would not be worth while to risk the blood of our people for *this*.

For it should scarcely seem questionable to anyone that even the restoration of the frontiers of 1914 could be achieved only by blood. Only childish and naïve minds can lull themselves in the idea that they can bring about a correction of Versailles by wheedling and begging. Quite aside from the fact that such an attempt would presuppose a man of Tallyrand's talents, which we do not possess. One half of our political figures consist of extremely sly, but equally spineless elements which are hostile toward our nation to begin with, while the other is composed of good-natured, harmless, and easy-going soft-heads. Moreover, the times have changed since the Congress of Vienna: *Today it is not princes and princes' mistresses who haggle and bargain over state borders; it is the inexorable Jew who struggles for his domination over the nations.* No nation can remove this hand from its throat except by the sword. Only the assembled and concentrated might of a national passion rearing up in its strength can defy the international enslavement of peoples. Such a process is and remains a bloody one.

If, however, we harbor the conviction that the German future, regardless what happens, demands the supreme sacrifice, quite aside from all considerations of political expediency as such, we must set up an aim worthy of this sacrifice and fight for it.

The boundaries of the year 1914 mean nothing at all for the German future. Neither did they provide a defense of the past, nor would they contain any strength for the future. Through them the German nation will neither achieve its inner integrity, nor will its sustenance be safeguarded by them, nor do these boundaries, viewed from the military standpoint, seem expedient or even satisfactory, nor finally can they improve the relation in which we at present

find ourselves toward the other world powers, or, better expressed, the real world powers. The lag behind England will not be caught up, the magnitude of the Union will not be achieved; not even France would experience a material diminution of her world-political importance.

Only one thing would be certain: even with a favorable outcome, such an attempt to restore the borders of 1914 would lead to a further bleeding of our national body, so much so that there would be no worth-while blood left to stake for the decisions and actions really to secure the nation's future. On the contrary, drunk with such a shallow success, we should renounce any further goals, all the more readily as "national honor" would be repaired and, for the moment at least, a few doors would have been reopened to commercial development.

As opposed to this, we National Socialists must hold unflinchingly to our aim in foreign policy, namely, *to secure for the German people the land and soil to which they are entitled on this earth.* And this action is the only one which, before God and our German posterity, would make any sacrifice of blood seem justified: before God, since we have been put on this earth with the mission of eternal struggle for our daily bread, beings who receive nothing as a gift, and who owe their position as lords of the earth only to the genius and the courage with which they can conquer and defend it; and before our German posterity in so far as we have shed no citizen's blood out of which a thousand others are not bequeathed to posterity. The soil on which some day German generations of peasants can beget powerful sons will sanction the investment of the sons of today, and will some day acquit the responsible statesmen of blood-guilt and sacrifice of the people, even if they are persecuted by their contemporaries.

And I must sharply attack those folkish pen-pushers who claim to regard such an acquisition of soil as a "breach of sacred human rights" and attack it as such in their scribblings. One never knows who stands behind these fellows. But one thing is certain, that the confusion they can create is desirable and convenient to our national enemies. By such an attitude they help to weaken and destroy from within our people's will for the only correct way of defending their vital needs. For no people on this earth possesses so much as a square yard of territory on the strength of a higher will or superior right. Just as Germany's frontiers are fortuitous frontiers, momentary frontiers in the current political struggle of any period, so are the boundaries of other nations' living space. And just as the shape of our earth's surface can seem immutable as granite only to the thoughtless soft-head, but in reality only represents at each period an apparent pause in a continuous development, created by the mighty forces of Nature in a process of continuous growth, only to be transformed or destroyed tomorrow by greater forces, likewise the boundaries of living spaces in the life of nations.

State boundaries are made by man and changed by man.

The fact that a nation has succeeded in acquiring an undue amount of soil constitutes no higher obligation that it should be recognized eternally. At most it proves the strength of the conquerors and the weakness of the nations. And in this case, right lies in this strength alone. If the German nation today, penned into an impossible area, faces a lamentable future, this is no more a commandment of Fate than revolt against this state of affairs constitutes an affront to Fate. No more than any higher power has promised another nation more territory than the German nation, or is offended by the fact of this unjust distribution of the soil. Just as our ancestors did not receive the soil on which we live today as a gift from Heaven, but had to fight for it at the risk of their lives, in the future no folkish grace will win

soil for us and hence life for our people, but only the might of a victorious sword.

Much as all of us today recognize the necessity of a reckoning with France, it would remain ineffectual in the long run if it represented the whole of our aim in foreign policy. It can and will achieve meaning only if it offers the rear cover for an enlargement of our people's living space in Europe. For it is not in colonial acquisitions that we must see the solution of this problem, but exclusively in the acquisition of a territory for settlement, which will enhance the area of the mother country, and hence not only keep the new settlers in the most intimate community with the land of their origin, but secure for the total area those advantages which lie in its unified magnitude.

The folkish movement must not be the champion of other peoples, but the vanguard fighter of its own. Otherwise it is superfluous and above all has no right to sulk about the past. For in that case it is behaving in exactly the same way. The old German policy was wrongly determined by dynastic considerations, and the future policy must not be directed by cosmopolitan folkish drivel. In particular, we are not constables guarding the well-known "poor little nations," but soldiers of our own nation.

But we National Socialists must go further. *The right to possess soil can become a duty if without extension of its soil a great nation seems doomed to destruction.* And most especially when not some little nigger nation or other is involved, but the Germanic mother of life, which has given the present-day world its cultural picture. *Germany will either be a world power or there will be no Germany.* And for world power she needs that magnitude which will give her the position she needs in the present period, and life to her citizens.

BULGARIA AND THE TREATY OF NEUILLY

Bulgarian grievances against the Treaty of Neuilly gained increasing momentum between the two world wars as a result of both official policy and a massive revisionist campaign launched in Bulgarian political publications. Georgi P. Genov was a leading spokesman for the revisionist movement. His summary of the nationalist case, reprinted below, was representative of widespread interwar Bulgarian opinion on the subject.

I N A brief statement such as the present, which of necessity is restricted both in extent and in the limits of the task undertaken, it is quite impossible to consider, estimate, and criticize all the decisions of the Treaty of Neuilly, which in itself is a great work of 296 pages treating of a vast number and varied and important matters. The greater part of the decisions are strictly of a juridical, economic, or financial character, and can hardly be made the subject of a statement like the present. The examination of all the clauses of a treaty of this kind demands a strictly scientific exposition, which in this case cannot be made in its full extent.

My task, therefore, has been more modest and limited. I have tried to give a general view of the conditions under which the Treaty of Neuilly was signed, the most significant of its provisions, and the ruinous results which it has had for Bulgaria, just as the other peace treaties had for the other vanquished countries.

With regard to the Treaty of Neuilly we may say in conclusion that many of its provisions, when examined from the point of view of international law, are shown to have been imposed without regard to right; while others, although in agreement with the principles of justice, are beyond the possibility of fulfillment.

The terms of the peace treaties were prepared in the period after the war, when lack of confidence and feelings of vengeance and hatred divided the nations into victors and vanquished. In view of existing psychological conditions among the allied powers and their statement one can understand why such burdensome and impossible conditions were prescribed in the treaties.

Fifteen years have passed since then. It is time to give a more correct estimation of the work of the Paris Conference. In so far as the provisions of the Treaty of Neuilly affect Bulgaria the results may be stated as follows:

(1) The Treaty of Neuilly confirmed and enforced the injustice done to Bulgaria at Bucharest in 1913. Purely Bulgarian lands, as Macedonia, Thrace, Dobrudia and the western border districts, remained within the frontiers of our neighbors by right of conquest.

(2) The national minorities of Bulgarian origin which remained in these and other provinces of neighboring states — notwithstanding the categorical stipulations of the treaties regarding the protection of minorities — have been deprived of personal security and property rights, and of elementary, cultural, educational, and religious rights and liberties, and have been subjected to a regime of violent denationalization and assimilation. They have been deprived of religious freedom and forbidden to speak in their mother tongue and to teach their children in their own national schools.

From Georgi P. Genov, *Bulgaria and the Treaty of Neuilly* (Sofia, 1935), pp. 182–186.

(3) Bulgaria remains fully disarmed, while all her neighbors are feverishly arming. The treaties disarmed the vanquished on the grounds of facilitating general disarmament. Fifteen years, however, have passed since the signature of this triumphant declaration, but general disarmament is still to come.

(4) All the vanquished countries, among which was Bulgaria, were burdened with colossal financial and other obligations. They could not have paid all that was asked of them. Besides, that which they have paid was beyond their ability to pay and has brought about their economic and financial ruin. The reparations were nothing less than the old military tribute. The claim that the principle of reparations is just because connected with the responsibility the treaties attempt to attribute to the conquered, is false.

(5) By Article 48 of the treaty, Bulgaria is promised an outlet to the Aegean Sea. So far it has not been granted. Our country has a commanding need of direct communication with the Mediterranean, which connects with the cultural West.

Bulgaria has looked upon the Treaty of Neuilly with great aversion because of the injustices done in it to our nation. It gave expression to this just aversion by the unanimous vote of its national representatives in the session of the National Assembly on November 9, 1919, when considering the proposed treaty of peace, which was signed later in Neuilly on the 27th of the same month. On this occasion the national representatives declared:

With feelings of extreme sorrow the National Assembly learns that the final decision of the great allied powers regarding the conditions of peace with Bulgaria remains unchanged.

All established principles of international justice and the free determination of nations are disregarded. The Bulgarian nation is punished with extreme cruelty.

Instead of the right of self-determination by plebiscite for parts of the Bulgarian nation within the boundaries of neighboring countries, new parts have been cut away from its main body and placed under foreign domination.

Instead of receiving a direct territorial outlet to the Aegean Sea, Bulgaria is deprived of her only port on that sea.

Instead of guaranteeing free political and economic life to our country, the treaty condemns Bulgaria to political and economic slavery.

Instead of peace, which should bring pacification in the Balkans, new pitfalls are dug, and the relations between the Balkan nations further poisoned.

Against such a peace the National Assembly considers that its duty, at this tragic moment, is to raise its voice once more in protest in the name of the entire Bulgarian nation.

In the name of historical justice, in the name of the often declared principles of liberty and justice even to the weak, in the name of millions of innocent Bulgarians who have a right to live their own national life, the National Assembly protests against this peace of injustice, and, leaving to the government the responsibility for further measures for the protection of the interests of Bulgaria, passes to the order of the day.

So far Bulgaria continues to live under the regime of the Treaty of Neuilly. The Bulgarian nation, however, has never recognized the validity of this treaty. In agreement with the protest of the National Assembly as expressed above, it does not cease to look upon the decision of the Paris Conference as unjust and harsh, and it awaits with faith and impatience the day when this work will destroy itself. Such outrageous slavery cannot be everlasting.

Peace in Europe will not be secured as long as the cruel and unjust treaties, such as the Paris Conference has given to the vanquished nations, are maintained: it will be secured only when a peaceful revision is achieved. Peace cannot rest upon force, injustice and social misery. Peace will be established when order has been reestablished upon the basis of right and justice. Such peace we shall have only when the Paris treaties are revised, and when the provisions of Article 19 of the pact of the League of Nations is put in force.

HUNGARY AND THE TREATY OF TRIANON

FRANCIS DEAK

In the decade following the signing of the Hungarian peace treaty of June, 1920, Hungarian political writings abounded with nationalist attacks on the treaty and impassioned pleas for its revision. In the late 1930's Professor Deak, an American scholar of Hungarian origin, undertook a thorough study of the Hungarian settlement which resulted in the first objective and scholarly account of the making of the Treaty of Trianon. Critical of the treaty's severity, Deak's conclusions, reprinted below, are based on extensive research and personal contact with leading personalities of Allied countries as well as Hungary.

THE STUDENT trying to assay the making of the Treaty of Trianon in the light of the record disclosed in the preceding pages has many pitfalls to avoid. The greatest difficulty lies in the inclination to make an appraisal in retrospect, in view of all the experiences of the intervening years, and then to apply the results as though the appraisal had been made contemporaneously. Whether praise for wisdom or criticism for the lack of foresight, the judgment thus made assumes that the makers of the treaty, as well as those who opposed and sought to change it, possessed the knowledge which, in the course of twenty years, has now become available to us.

Another difficulty is presented by the pragmatic approach, which unfortunately had been predominant for the last twenty-five years in all social sciences, but quite particularly so in the field of international relations. The great drawback of the pragmatic approach lies in its oversimplification of causes; major movements in the evolution of society, national and international, and particularly the balance between peace and war, are compressed as though springing from single causes, such as the struggle for raw materials, or overpopulation. The eco-nomic factor is almost always predominant. Nowhere has this tendency been more evident and its results more overpowering than in the case of the peace treaties of 1919–1920. The Germans, in particular, attributed all their ills solely and exclusively to the Treaty of Versailles, although Professor Shotwell demonstrated strikingly in his *What Germany Forgot* how misleading such an assumption was. Yet the thesis was accepted in Germany without reservation; and the Germans almost succeeded in convincing the rest of the world that the disintegration of Europe was caused largely if not exclusively by the inequities of the Treaty of Versailles. The Hungarians, who had to make sacrifices so much greater and whose national existence was so much more profoundly affected by the peace settlement than that of the Germans, have likewise regarded the Treaty of Trianon as the chief if not the only source of their sufferings and hardships since 1920.

Constructive criticism of the peace treaties must proceed on a broader basis. It should take into account the fact that the forces producing major transformations in society are too numerous and too complex to be identified with a single factor or phe-

From Francis Deak, *Hungary at the Paris Peace Conference* (New York, 1942), pp. 343–352. Reprinted by permission of the Carnegie Endowment for International Peace.

nomenon. As Professor Shotwell pointed out in the Foreword to this volume, the corrosive forces which destroyed European equilibrium were in operation long before the inadequacy of the peace treaties gave those forces greater striking power. Looking therefore at events in their historical perspective, Europe's bankruptcy must be attributed to something more fundamental and less tangible than the mistakes of the peace settlement.

Constructive criticism also should avoid basing conclusions on the letter of any treaty and should take account of the spirit and intent with which it is carried out. Even an imperfect treaty — and surely no political treaty was ever regarded by all of the co-contractants as perfect — could accomplish a desired end for the benefit of all, if applied wisely, with foresight and restraint. This is in no way different from the success or the failure of laws and institutions in the domestic life of nations, which depends not on the letter but on the spirit in which they are administered. Conversely, a treaty, or law, or institution, satisfying the highest standards of ethics or the most exacting principles of abstract justice, may bring disaster in its wake if its administration is characterized by inflexibility and shortsightedness. It is on this score that the peace treaties of 1919-20, and particularly the treaty with Hungary, can be subjected to severe criticism. But this is beyond the scope of our task.

With all these caveats in mind, there is still little praise for the Treaty of Trianon as an instrument of peace. In passing judgment, one need not adopt the bitterly critical point of view of the Hungarians. Their attitude is generated not only by the conviction that the provisions of the treaty — particularly the dismemberment of their country and the allocation of large numbers of Magyars to alien rulers — were unjust and inequitable. Their resentment was accentuated by the feeling that the treaty was made unilaterally, upon the presentation of *ex parte* evidence by Hungary's ad-

versaries, and without adequate opportunity for rebuttal. So much for the Hungarian point of view.

Without necessarily subscribing to the Hungarian thesis in its entirety or to the charge of ill will toward Hungary on the part of the framers of the treaty (a charge readily made in all sincerity by Hungarians), it must be conceded that the decisions incorporated in that document were arrived at by processes inconsistent with the rule of the *audiatur et altera pars;* and that, in substance, they fell far short of the principles and objectives proclaimed by the Allies. To be sure, this conclusion is not to be confined to the Treaty of Trianon alone, but is equally pertinent in regard to all the peace treaties drawn up in 1919. The correctness of this conclusion may be tested by comparing the results of the treaties with Germany, Austria, Bulgaria, and Hungary — all completed by unilateral procedure — with those of the Treaty of Lausanne with Turkey, which was preceded by negotiations. In fairness it should be pointed out that the procedure followed at the Paris Peace Conference was not a preconceived one, for the original plan contemplated negotiations on the final peace terms with the ex-enemy states after the imposition of the armistice conditions and the establishment of a "preliminary" peace. Unless it is conceded that the Allies did envisage a negotiated peace, much of President Wilson's Fourteen Points would have to be regarded as meaningless. The great difference between the approach to the peace settlements as originally conceived and as actually practiced is strikingly illustrated by a confidential British document prepared, apparently, as a guide for the British peace negotiators.

The introductory paragraphs of this document state that as regards the European Continent, Great Britain had no territorial ambitions or special commercial interests. "Our general object must be the establishment of a stable condition. . . . What we want is peace and order with open facilities for trade." Pointing out that general questions regarding Europe fell into two main categories, namely, territorial redistribution and guarantees for free international trade, the memorandum expressed the view that territorial questions were almost entirely confined to Eastern Europe, since boundaries in the West were settled permanently and satisfactorily after the question of Alsace-Lorraine had been adjusted. The memorandum then continues:

10. The East of Europe has not yet attained this condition; ultimately, this is one of the chief causes of the present war and no League of Nations can avoid future wars until this condition has been established there also. The establishment of this condition will, so far as it is possible, be the work of the Peace Conference. *In Eastern Europe, therefore, the territorial problem is that which will assume the first importance, and the future peace of the world will depend on the method in which this is settled. No settlement can be stable and permanent unless it is just. It is of the highest importance that no well-founded sense of injustice should be allowed to remain* and, to use President Wilson's words, "we must be just towards those whom we should wish not to be just." The Germans in Bohemia and the Magyars must be treated on exactly the same principle as the Czechs and the Roumanians.

Since England had no direct interest in these questions, the memorandum suggested that the British Government could exert a strong influence as a disinterested and impartial arbitrator. "Our object should be that when the whole transaction is concluded, all these nations, Czecho-Slovaks, Jugo-Slavs, Poles — we may perhaps add even Bulgarians, Magyars, and Germans — will feel that on the part of the British nation there has been an honest attempt to carry through a disinterested policy which has sought to represent the best interests of all, for, in the long run, the interests of each nation are not antagonistic to those of the other nations."

With respect to procedure, the memorandum counseled against taking the initiative and advocated intervention only if the parties directly concerned should not be able to agree:

14. The procedure to be adopted should be that all the individual States concerned should be informed that the Allies would look to them to consider the frontiers which should be assigned to them in each case, and *to enter into negotiations with the other States concerned.** It is hoped that by negotiation and discussion a friendly agreement may be made. The final decision will, of course, be reserved for the Peace Conference. If an agreement has been arrived at by the States themselves, then presumably little would remain in such cases except for the Peace Conference to ratify the decision. If no agreement has been made, then the Peace Conference would consider the matter, and determine it in the form of an arbitration, but their determination would be final, and would, if necessary, be enforced by arms.

No argument is necessary to show that the recommendations, whether substantive or procedural, contained in this British memorandum have not been followed, although the assumptions upon which these recommendations were predicated were sound, as subsequent developments have proved. Failure to proceed according to the Wilsonian principles and the British suggestion may be explained but hardly excused by circumstances prevailing in 1919 — the war-weariness in the Allied countries and the resulting pressure to "get done" with the peace settlement, the controversies between the Allies, the turn of sentiment in the United States which impaired the influence the Americans might otherwise have exercised, and other known factors which induced haste. The result was, as we know today and as thoughtful observers have realized for some time past, a settlement which was, at least in the eyes of large sections of Europe and elsewhere, not just and consequently not stable. The greatest dissatisfaction and the bitterest denunciation of the peace settlements came from the Hungarians who looked upon the Treaty

* Author's italics.

of Trianon, it seems, with more intense feeling of injustice than that with which the Germans, Austrians, or Bulgarians received their respective treaties. The intensity of the feelings of the Hungarians was beyond doubt due largely to the magnitude of their losses — losses measured not merely in terms of square miles of territory but also in agricultural and industrial resources.

Yet, making full allowance for the Hungarians, the main criticism ought to be directed not against the injustices inflicted on the Hungarian people and not against the Treaty of Trianon as such, but rather toward the failure of the Peace Conference to deal realistically and constructively with the problem of European peace as an indivisible whole. Looking at the matter from this angle, the Treaty of Trianon becomes merely one of several pillars — though a rather important one — in a defective architectural plan; and the complaints of the Hungarians merely one of several outstanding examples of the results of the defects.

How can this failure be explained? Was the stature of the statesmen assembled in Paris smaller than of those who drew up, a century before, the Act of Vienna? I believe that such would be an unwarranted judgment. Had there been inadequate preparation? Never before had science and scholarship been called upon so much to the preparation of a peace treaty as in 1919; never before on such an occasion had statesmen been assisted by such an array of distinguished experts and technicians. The details were worked out painstakingly and in most instances, conscientiously; but how solid was the framework into which these details had to be fitted? How lasting the foundation upon which the framework itself was to rest?

In the past, treaties of peace were par excellence political treaties; the peace treaties at the end of the first World War were, with the exception of the Treaty of Lausanne, dominated by considerations of a moral character, in anticipation of an international society to be governed by a wholly new set of principles. The plan of President Wilson for the League of Nations which prefaced the peace treaties was devised and intended to embody this new international society. It was the most daring suggestion ever advanced for the orderly conduct of international relations; a suggestion which challenged the imagination of mankind as never anything before or since. The peace settlement was built on the fundamental assumption that it would operate in an international society, bound together in the League, and that the conduct of its members would be in conformity with the principles embodied in its Covenant. Inherent in and underlying this assumption was the expectation, at least on the part of the Americans, that inequities in the settlement would be gradually cured through the orderly processes of negotiations.

Unfortunately, the world was not ready for this revolutionary innovation. As far as Europe was concerned, the innovation, if successful, would have served as a substitute for the "balance of power." This system has always had a sinister implication for many people and, more particularly, for Americans, perhaps because their attention was focused on its dramatic failures, ignoring its less spectacular accomplishments. Nevertheless, the balance of power was more often than not a useful, indeed an indispensable instrument for the maintenance of Continental equilibrium in the face of constantly shifting forces. It had been the most constant political reality in European diplomatic history since the rise of the national state. Peace itself is of course nothing more, nor less, than a delicately balanced equilibrium of conflicting national interests — an equilibrium which insures that the forces on the side of stability, order, and peaceful evolution are evenly matched against single or concerted aspirations for revolutionary change. The balance of power, despite all its defects, was merely the application of this process to the peculiar conditions of the European Continent. It is true that with the disintegration of the Austro-Hungarian Monarchy one of the vital pillars supporting the balance disappeared; and that another vital arch in the system, Russia, engulfed in Bolshevism, did not appeal to the Peace Conference as being an acceptable partner in the concert of Europe. Therefore the abandonment of the balance of power by the Peace Conference is in itself understandable.

A wholly different question is whether there was political realism in anticipating that the League of Nations could accomplish in a larger area what the balance of power could not do within the confines of Europe. The answer to this question, especially in relation to Southeastern and Eastern Europe, must be in the negative. In dealing with those areas the Peace Conference seems to have ignored two essential considerations. In the first place, the great importance of the Middle Danube basin in the interplay of European politics was overlooked. Whether from the economic or the strategic point of view, this importance could hardly be exaggerated. In the second place, no account was taken of the forces which would pit the small nations, successors of the Austro-Hungarian Monarchy, against each other — forces which were more likely to operate centripetally and centrifugally.

Even under the Monarchy these centripetal forces had been strong enough to prevent a genuine federalism and had been the cause of much factional dispute. It was therefore inevitable that if the framework of Empire and Kingdom was dissolved without some adequate substitute, there would be something approaching anarchy in the international relations of the Succession States. The framers of the peace treaties must therefore bear at least the initial responsibility for having brought about these conditions without an adequate safeguard against their consequences.

The political chaos which was bound to plague Europe, and perhaps the world, was foreseen by very few at that time. There is one notable exception: the distinguished French historian, Jacques Bainville, member of the *Académie Française,* in a remarkable though little known book, published in 1920, pointed out the political shortcomings of the peace settlement and predicted, with uncanny accuracy, its political consequences.* M. Bainville, although concentrating primarily on the treaty with Germany, viewed the problems of the whole Continent. He found the cardinal error in the fact that the Treaty of Versailles left German unity unimpaired, while the aggregate effect of the peace settlements was bound further to consolidate this unity internally and to open the road for further expansion externally by destroying and dissipating the barriers which could have stemmed such expansion.

One of the important barriers in the past was the Austro-Hungarian Monarchy, which dissolved as a result of the war. Its disintegration was confirmed by the Peace Conference in the treaties with Austria and Hungary. Conceding that the Monarchy was too antiquated to justify resuscitation, the question still remains whether the Peace Conference should not have foreseen the necessity of a substitute, by some combination of the Succession States, which could serve as a politically, economically, and militarily equivalent heir to the defunct Monarchy, to bar the *Drang nach Osten.* Instead, after having concluded that a composite empire like Austria-Hungary ought not to exist, the Peace Conference created Czecho-Slovakia, surrounded on three sides by a compact mass of Germans and composed of five of the eight nationalities which lived in the former Monarchy. Instead, a truncated state of Germanic people was enjoined to lead an independent national existence under the name of Austria, although a little foresight should have made evident the irresistible appeal which the neighboring Reich would exert; should have

* *Les Consequences politiques de la paix.* The author stated in his preface that he did not write the book as an answer to Mr. Keynes's *Economic Consequences of the Peace,* which had appeared and had created a sensation a few months earlier. Nothing illustrates more clearly the a-political thinking of the period between the two world wars than the fact that M. Bainville's book, as prophetic in the political field as Mr. Keynes's in the economic, remained practically unnoticed.

shown that once Vienna became part of that Reich, Czecho-Slovakia was lost; and that having crossed the Carpathians, the road was open for the Germans down to the Black Sea and the Mediterranean, for neither Hungary, nor Yugoslavia, nor Rumania, nor Bulgaria could resist, either singly or even jointly.

The key to European peace had lain, at least since the Treaty of Westphalia, in the rule that no single nation ought to be allowed to dominate the Continent. True, wars had to be fought to enforce the rule; but these wars were decidedly on the decrease in the nineteenth century. As a matter of fact, adherence to this rule was one of the few immutable principles of the otherwise flexible and adaptable British foreign policy. It should have been a paramount consideration also at the Peace Conference, especially since the unification of Germany and its geographical position in the center of the Continent, together with the rapid growth of its population and its industrial development, made that country more than any other European power (with the possible exception of Russia) likely to impair the rule. Taking into account the political history of the nineteenth and early twentieth century, the unalterable geographic factors, and the lessons of trade and communications, then the vital importance of the Middle Danube basin as the corner stone of European equilibrium, whether threatened by Germany in the near future or by Russia in a somewhat more distant future, ought not to have escaped attention and should have received the most thoughtful examination of the statesmen assembled in Paris.

It is perhaps true that by an appreciation of the dangers which each of the new states in Southeastern Europe faced and through the application of wise statesmanship by the leaders of these states, much of the short-sightedness of the peace settlements might have been cured and many, if not all, of its tragic consequences avoided. It is possible that if the hope of a truly great statesman — that of the late President Masaryk of Czecho-Slovakia — had been possible of realization, the second world war could have been avoided. President Masaryk dreamed of a relationship between the new states in Southeastern Europe based on the principles of Jeffersonian democracy, transplanted from the United States to the banks of the Danube. How little the peoples of Southeastern Europe were ready to accept such principles in their dealings with each other is conclusively shown by the fact that the integral application and operation of them proved to be impossible, even in President Masaryk's own country. Thus the mistakes of the peace settlement, far from having been remedied in the succeeding years, as both President Wilson and President Masaryk had hoped and expected, were accentuated by the absence of sufficiently constructive statesmanship to restrain the forces of nationalism. The responsibility lies not so heavily on the individuals whose names are customarily connected with historic events as it does on the nations in whose names they have spoken and acted. Neither is such responsibility to be charged particularly to any one nation; all people, on both sides of the fence, ought to bear a share proportionate to the influence they wielded or could have wielded. It may be that neither individuals nor nations can profit much by past experience; yet it is hard to believe that the same mistakes would be committed twice by the same generation. For that reason, this book may be concluded with the sincere hope that whatever errors may mark the next peace settlement, they will not be repetitions of those which characterized the treaties of 1919–20. By looking not at the next elections but at the prosperity and happiness of the next generation, many of the pitfalls can be avoided.

THE CASE FOR THE SUCCESSOR STATES

THOMAS GARRIGUE MASARYK

Son of a Moravian coachman on one of the Imperial Habsburg estates, Thomas Masaryk became the first President of Czechoslovakia in 1918. His extraordinary scholarly as well as political accomplishments rank him as probably the most outstanding philosopher and statesman of Eastern Europe in the immediate decades before and after World War I. His writings range over the fields of history, sociology, literary criticism, philosophy, and politics, while all his actions were directed to what he called the "moral and political education" of the Czechoslovak people. Well known in Western Europe and the United States (he was married to an American, Charlotte Garrigue), Masaryk successfully directed the Czechoslovak national movement in western capitals during World War I. His efforts, culminating in the proclamation of an independent Czechoslovak Republic in October, 1918, are described in his political memoirs, *The Making of a State,* from which the following passages are drawn. As a staunch defender of the territorial and political rearrangement of Eastern Europe, and of the principle of national self-determination, which he viewed as the harbinger of a new international morality, Masaryk emerged as a leading spokesman for the so-called Successor States.

THERE is much truth in the saying that States are preserved by the same political forces as those which engendered them. For this reason I shall sum up the story of our work abroad in a systematic account of its political and juridical significance, so as to show how our Republic arose and how we attained independence.

Generally speaking, our independence is a fruit of the fall of Austria-Hungary and of the world conflagration. In vanquishing Germany and Austria, the Allies won our freedom and made it possible. At the Peace Conference the victors established a new order in Western and Central Europe. We took part in these conferences from beginning to end and signed the Treaties, since the Allies, recognizing and accepting our programme of liberation, had admitted us during the war into the areopagus of belligerent nations in whose hands the decision lay. And our former enemies presently recognized our independence in their turn by signing and by giving constitutional ratification to the Peace Treaties.

Yet it was only by our resistance to Austria-Hungary and by our revolt against her that we earned our independence. As President Poincaré tersely said, we won it by fighting in France, Italy, and Russia. The peculiarity of our revolt lay in its not being carried through by force of arms on our own soil, but abroad, on foreign soil. As a people we were bound to take part in the war. Otherwise independence would not have been attained — assuredly not in the degree in which we attained it. Herein lie the meaning and the political value of our Legions in Russia, France, and Italy. They secured for us the goodwill and the help of the Western Powers, while the march through Siberia gained us the liking

From Thomas G. Masaryk, *The Making of a State* (London, 1927), pp. 333–336, 370–372, 385–390. Reprinted by permission of George Allen and Unwin, Ltd.

of the Allied public at large and the respect even of our enemies.

Together with the Legions, those of our soldiers who helped to break up the Austrian Army by active and passive resistance lent essential aid to the cause, especially those who, in resisting, forfeited their lives. Every execution of such men dug deeper the grave of the authorities in Vienna and Budapest, for it proved that our people was locked in a life and death struggle with them. And every such execution we brought to public knowledge abroad, arraigning Austria openly and charging her with persecution and cruelty. In the young sculptor Šapík the spirit of the people was finely revealed. Mobilized and sent to the Russian front, he said, in bidding farewell to his friends at Prague, "I know I shall fall, but I will fire no shot against Russia." Hardly had he reached the front when he fell — having kept his word. Of such as he there were many thousands. The civilians, too, who were executed under the Austrian military terror; or who, like Dr. Kramář and Dr. Rašín, were condemned to death and imprisoned; and those whose property was confiscated or who were made to suffer in other ways, all bore their part in the work of liberation — they and the nameless souls in all classes of the Czech people for whom Austrian persecution made bitterer still the bitter time of war. Our freedom was truly bought with blood.

Other factors in the struggle were the diplomatic action and the propaganda of our National Council abroad. We formed the Legions, developed them into an army, and turned their share in the war to political account. The National Council abroad was the organ of men at home who discerned the nature of the world war and took the fatal decision either to carry on our revolt in foreign countries or to support it effectively by subterranean action at home. Everywhere, even in Russia, the main task was to break down traditional pro-Austrianism; and in this we succeeded.

We, who were abroad, managed besides to convince the Allies of our historical and natural right to independence. We revealed to them the true character of the Hapsburg absolutism. We showed that, under cover of constitutional appearances, a minority ruled over a majority in Austria-Hungary and that things in Austria and Hungary were as anachronistic and anomalous as was the Caesarism of Prussia and Russia. This the Western peoples understood as regards Prussia and Russia, and it was our business to persuade them that the Caesarism of Vienna was no better, nay, in many respects, worse. We dwelt upon the cruelty of Austria toward those of her peoples who were not of her mind, upon her dependence on Germany and pan-German policy, and upon her heavy share of war guilt; and, by showing what part our people had taken in the development of European culture, we justified our claim to independence. Even among the masses of the Allied peoples our four years' propaganda spread these truths and drove them home.

Pro-Austrianism did not consist merely of a liking for Austria and Vienna, but was inspired by the traditional view that Austria was a dam against Germany; and though the war was in itself a refutation of this view, it still prevailed. As I have shown, it was very strong in all Allied and neutral countries, and it was no easy matter to overcome it, the less easy because many of us had long sought to persuade the world that Austria was a necessity. Besides, an intense pro-Austrian propaganda worked against us. Our victory was therefore the more remarkable. The Allies knew less than we about Austria-Hungary, and they were totally unacquainted with the complicated racial and economic conditions in Eastern Europe. Our long experience and study of Eastern Europe enabled us therefore to put forward a positively-conceived policy against Austria and Germany. Indeed, as I have said in referring to my first official interview with Briand, we supplied the Allies with a political programme. This is no exaggeration, as our friends in France, England, and America admit. Nor did we give them only our programme. We gave them programmes for the liberation of other peoples and for the reconstruction of Europe as a whole. Of this, proof may be found in my work "The New Europe" which was handed in French and English to all the Allied delegates to the Peace Conferences at the end of the war.

* * *

Big peoples, like the British and the American, who are wont to apply continental standards of judgment and are not greatly troubled by questions of language, are wont to look upon the liberation of small peoples and the creation of small States as a bothersome process of political and linguistic "Balkanization." Yet circumstances are what they are, determined by Nature and History. Turkey, Austria-Hungary, Germany, and Russia simplified half of Europe by methods of violence, mechanically, and therefore, temporarily. As remedies for "Balkanization," freedom and democracy are preferable.

The problem is whether the big peoples which have hitherto threatened the small peoples and each other will accept the principle that all nations, big and small, are equally entitled to their own individualities in political organization and in culture. Recent political evolution has been favourable to the little peoples. Against a German mastery over Europe the whole world rose in self-defence. The Allies proclaimed the principle of equal rights for small nations, and President Wilson defended those rights with his watchword "self-determination." The Peace Treaties codified the fundamental features of this idea. True, the old jealousies between the Great Powers are not yet removed; and new causes of bitterness have been added to the old, bitterness engendered by defeat and by the nonfulfilment of some of the victors' wishes and purposes. Nevertheless the Peace Treaties have created juster conditions throughout Europe, and we are entitled to expect that the tension between States and races will decrease.

Despite all antagonisms, there is, moreover, ground for hope that the lessons of the war will strengthen the prospects of peace. What may be faulty in the new order will be susceptible of pacific adjustment as occasion arises. All difficulties notwithstanding, it is possible to detect the beginnings of a free federalization of Europe in place of the absolutist mastery of one Great Power or of alliances of Great Powers, over the Continent. In a new Europe of this kind the independence of even the smallest national individuality can be safeguarded; and the League of Nations suggests an instructive analogy to what a united Europe may become.

Before the war, doubt was long and often felt whether our nation or any small nation could be independent — the doubt which inspired Palacký's well-known saying that Austria was necessary as a federation of races. Great as is my deference to Palacký, and carefully though I have ever borne in mind the difficulties and the special problems of little peoples, I believed nevertheless our own independence to be possible. This belief engendered my whole policy and tactics. It moved me during the war to begin the struggle against Austria-Hungary. I held our independence feasible on condition that we should always be ready and be morally fit — as Havlíček demanded — to defend our freedom, that we should possess enough political understanding to follow an honest and reasonable policy at home and abroad, and that we should win sympathies in a democratically strengthened Europe. If the democratic principle prevails all round, one nation cannot suppress another. The history of Europe since the eighteenth century proves that, given democratic freedom, little peoples can gain independence. The World War was the climax of the movement begun by the French Revolution, a movement that liberated one oppressed people after another, and now there is a chance for a democratic Europe and for the freedom and independence of all her nations.

* * *

In some degree our foreign policy is determined by regard for our racial minorities.

Save in the smallest States such minorities exist, inasmuch as a strictly ethnographical delimitation of frontiers is impracticable. Nationality, as expressed in terms of race, played little or no part in the formation of the majority of existing States. Indeed, the principle of nationality acquired State-creative power only in the modern era and, even then, it was not alone decisive.

No two minority questions are alike. Each presents peculiarities of its own. Our German minority in Czechoslovakia is a case in point. It is comparatively large, for it numbers three millions out of a total population of thirteen. Eleven European States count fewer than three million inhabitants. Our Germans are, moreover, mature in culture and are economically, industrially and financially strong. Politically, they suffer from the drawback that, under Austria, the Vienna Government looked after them to such an extent that their own political sense was not whetted. But at their back stands the great German people, and they are neighbours of Austria who is a neighbour of Germany.

Our claim that the German minority should remain with us is based on our historic right and on the fact that the Germans of Bohemia never attached value to union with Germany while they were under Austrian rule, or even in the time of the Bohemian Kingdom. It was modern pan-German propaganda that first gained adherents among them. During the war they sided with Austria and Germany against us. After the war, and particularly after the revolution in Prague, they sought to organize their own territory politically, but the very attempt proved the impossibility of coordinating their scattered and disconnected regions under one administration. The fact that they set up a variety of German units speaks for itself.

A Czech proposal, which was taken into consideration at the Peace Conference, was once made to cede a part of German Bohemia to Germany. The idea of delimiting the new States as far as possible according to nationality had no lack of supporters in England and America. Yet, on mature reflection, many political men with whom I discussed it, recognized that the discontinuity of important sections of our German territory, no less than its economic interests, told in favour of our historic right; and, at the Peace Conference, these considerations prevailed.

Soberly judged, it is to the interest of our Germans themselves that there should be more rather than fewer of them among us. Were we to cede one and a half or even two millions of them to Germany, the remaining million would have far greater reason to fear Czechization than the three millions fear it now. And, if we consider the position between us and our Germans as it was under Austria and as the pan-Germans would like to have it today, the question arises whether it is fairer that a fragment of the German people should remain in a non-German State or that the whole Czechoslovak people should live in a German State.

The authority of President Wilson and the principle of self-determination have been invoked by our own Germans as well as by those of Austria. True, "self-determination" was not recognized in Germany, nor did Austrian Germans like Dr. Lammasch, Dr. Redlich, and others admit it, not to mention Czernin and other Austro-Hungarian Ministers. Before the war our people, too, proclaimed it; but, in point of fact, it has never been clearly defined. Does it apply only to a whole people or is it valid also for sections of a people? A minority, even a big minority, is not a nation. Nor does "self-determination" carry with it an unconditional right to political independence. Our Germans may "determine" to remain with us, as the Swiss Germans have "determined" to stay outside Germany. Individual rights are not the sole governing factors in the question whether a whole, or parts of a whole, shall be independent; the rights of others enter into it, economic rights no less than the claims of race and tongue; and in our case, Czech rights as well as German, and considerations of reciprocal advantage, especially in the economic sphere.

Hence it was urged at the Peace Conference that to exclude the German minority from Bohemia would damage the Czech majority — a decision the more warranted because the German people in general derives great political benefit, greater than it would if it were wholly united, from the circumstance that a notable part of it lives outside Germany proper, forming an independent State in Austria, holding a preponderant position in Switzerland, and possessing minorities in Czechoslovakia and elsewhere. Even since the war a number of German political men and historians have, indeed, proved that, from the standpoint of culture, the German people gains by its membership of different States. The same reasoning applies to the French — in France, Belgium, and Switzerland — and to the English. Naturally, the Germans outside Germany are entitled to political freedom and to a due share in the administration of the States to which they belong. Those States, for their part, are entitled to demand that their German citizens shall not be an aggressive vanguard, as the pan-Germans would have them be, and that they should make up their minds to work together in peace with the peoples among whom they have lived for centuries and to whom they are bound by ties material and spiritual.

Our Germans, as I pointed out in my first Presidential Message, originally came to us as colonists; and the significance of this German colonization would not be lessened even if it were true that a few Germans were already living in the country. Yet this does not mean that, as colonists, our Germans are second-class citizens. They were invited to come by our Kings who guaranteed to them the right to live their own lives in full measure — a weighty circumstance, politically and tactically, for the Germans as well as for us. I, for my part, acknowledge and deliberately adopt the policy of our Přemyslide Kings who protected the Germans as a race, though I do not approve of the Germanophil leanings of some of the Přemyslides. I have nothing against the association of the name "Přemyslide" — which, from our verb přemysliti, means "thoughtful" — with the Greek Prometheus, but rather perceive in the name of our first dynasty a reminder that our whole policy, not alone in regard to the Germans, must be well-pondered, thoroughly thought out or, as Havlíček demanded, reasonable and upright. The settlement of the conflict between us and our Germans will be a great political deed, for it implies the solution of a question centuries old, the ordering of our relationship to a large section of the German people and, through it, to the German people as a whole. To this end our Germans must de-Austrianize themselves and get rid of the old habit of mastery and privilege.

Politically, the Germans are the most important of our minorities, and their acceptance of our Republic will simplify all the other minority questions. Alongside of the Germans we have a few Poles, more Little Russians (in Slovakia) and still more Magyars. To them also the rule applies that the rights of race must be safeguarded. Local self-government and proportional representation may, in a democratic State, serve this purpose well. Each minority, too, must have elementary and secondary schools of its own. In civilized Europe the number of high schools and universities is now determined by a definite ratio to population and educational needs. In Germany there are approximately one university for every three million and a technical high school for every six million inhabitants. In Czechoslovakia three million Germans have a university and two technical schools.

For us, who live in a country racially mixed and so curiously situated in the centre of Europe, the language question is of great moment, politically and educationally. The official language in a multi-lingual State must be determined by the requirements of the people and by the smooth working of the administration. The State exists for the people, not the people for the State. As a political entity and a unitary organization, our State and its army will use the Czech or Slovak language in accordance with the democratic principle that the majority decides. But, while the State will be Czechoslovak, its racial character cannot be settled by the official language alone. National character does not depend solely on language; and the national character of our State must be based upon the quality of a comprehensive educational policy consistently pursued.

Before the war I took part in the controversy upon the question whether the authorities should be unilingual or bi-lingual. In present circumstances I think it more practical that they should be bi-lingual though, during the transition period, it may be better, in some bi-lingual offices, that officials should work in one language only. Experience will presently show whether a unilingual system is feasible. In practice the question is one of knowing the languages spoken in the country. It is in the interest of racial minorities to learn the State language, but it is also in the interest of the majority to be able to speak the languages of the minorities, especially that of the biggest minority. The teaching of languages in the schools will be arranged on this basis. The German language is politically important for us. Our officials must know it, and know it well so as to understand even popular dialects. German is a world-language; and, if only on this account, is valuable as a means of education and culture. German must be taught in the Czech and Slovak secondary schools and in the higher classes of the elementary schools. In the corresponding German schools, Czech must be taught. In Slovakia an analogous rule applies, though perhaps to a more limited extent, to Slovak and Magyar. Time and experience will show whether the learning of these languages should be made compulsory or not. It must be remembered, if the complexity of our language question is to be understood, that in addition to our home languages we need Latin and Greek in our Classical high schools besides a knowledge of French and English,

Russian and Italian. If they are true sons of Comenius, our pedagogues will have to simplify and to perfect our methods of teaching, so that the learning of languages may be made as easy as possible.

Chauvinism is nowhere justified, least of all in our country. A noteworthy fact, which I often mention to Germans and foreigners as characteristic of our people and of our revolution, is that despite all the Austrian acts of oppression during the war and the intolerant demeanour of a large number of our Germans, no violence was done to the Germans in Prague or elsewhere on October 28, 1918. So filled were our folk with the positive idea of creating a State that they thought no evil and took no reprisals. One or two excesses on the part of individuals prove nothing to the contrary. From the first, the leaders of the revolution wished the Germans to cooperate with them; and, at the Geneva Conference between the delegates of the Prague National Committee and Dr. Beneš a proposal was adopted without discussion, as something self-evident, that a German Minister should be included in the Government. In a democracy it is obviously the right of every party to share in the administration of the State as soon as it recognizes the policy of the State and the State itself. Nay, it is its duty to share in it. I know further that the National Committee in Prague simultaneously negotiated with the Germans and sought to gain their goodwill. The Germans affirm that the Lord Lieutenant of Bohemia, Count Coudenhove, was asked on October 29 to join the National Committee as a German representative. In the same spirit our National Committee at Brno, or Brüun, promised the military command in Moravia to invite two Germans to join it. After the revolution, the Czech leaders offered to set up a special Department of State for German affairs — a conciliatory and far-sighted step.

Chauvinism, that is to say, political, religious, racial, or class intolerance, has as history proves, wrought the downfall of all States. A modern Portuguese historian whose name I forget but whom I read in London, shows convincingly that chauvinistic imperialism wrecked the Portuguese World-Empire. The same lesson is taught by the fall of Austria and Hungary, Prussia-Germany and Russia — they who take the sword shall perish by the sword. We shall solve our own problem aright if we comprehend that the more humane we are the more national we shall be. The relationship between the nation and mankind, between nationality and internationality, between nationalism and humaneness of feeling is not that mankind as a whole and internationalism and humaneness are something apart from, against or above the nation and nationality, but that nations are the natural organs of mankind. The new order in Europe, the creation of new States, has shorn nationalism of its negative character by setting oppressed peoples on their own feet. To a positive nationalism, one that seeks to raise a nation by intensive work, none can demur. Chauvinism, racial or national intolerance, not love of one's own people, is the foe of nations and of humanity. Love of one's own nation does not entail non-love of other nations.

It is natural that, as a general rule, nationality should be determined by language, for language is an expression, albeit not the only expression of the national spirit. Since the eighteenth century, students of nationality have recognized that it is expressed rather in the whole of a nation's intellectual effort and culture. Conscious fostering of nationality implies therefore a comprehensive policy of culture and education. Literature and art, philosophy and science, legislation and the State, politics and administration, moral, religious, and intellectual style, have to be national. Now that we have won political independence and are masters of our fate, a policy conceived in the days of our bondage can no longer suffice. Emphasis was then laid upon our linguistic claims. Now our national programme must embrace the whole domain of culture. To the synthesis of culture towards which educated Europe is now striving, I have already referred. It is in countries of mixed race that this synthesis can best begin; and to all racial minorities among educated peoples a weighty and honourable task is thus assigned.

GEOGRAPHY, JUSTICE, AND POLITICS
AT THE PARIS CONFERENCE OF 1919

CHARLES SEYMOUR

A close associate of Colonel House, Charles Seymour headed the Austro-Hungarian Division of the American Commission to Negotiate Peace in 1919 and also served as a United States delegate on the Czechoslovak, Rumanian, and Yugoslav territorial commissions. He authored a number of significant studies of Woodrow Wilson and American diplomacy during World War I and edited, prior to becoming President of Yale University, *The Intimate Papers of Colonel House*. Invited to deliver the first Bowman Memorial Lecture in 1951, under the joint auspices of the American Geographical Society and The Johns Hopkins University, he took a new hard look at the interplay of geography, justice, and politics as the determining factors in the making of the Peace of Versailles.

THE PARIS Conference of 1919 was not an isolated event in history, without relationship to what had preceded or would follow. As the biographer of Lord Balfour tells us, he "thought of the Conference less as the beginning of a new order or as the end of an old one than as a point in time whose realities would be no more static than time itself."

At the very outset of his monumental description of "The New World," Isaiah Bowman warns us to be careful in our assumptions of the connotations of the word "New." "Shaken vitally out of their former routine," he writes, "people have everywhere created or adopted new ideas and new material arrangements. Yet the student of history sees in this period of change but a step in our age-old process; to him the effects of the war are as new ingredients dropped into the caldron of humanity." (Let us note that Dr. Bowman speaks of new ingredients but not of new dynamics.) "The world is not new," he continues, "in the sense that war has ceased, that all political and social problems will be promptly settled, that present international boundaries and economic arrangements will forever remain unchanged. . . . Men's mental qualities and reactions change but little; they repeat certain effects from age to age. Almost every event of our time has its counterpart in history."

Thus the major factors determining a peace settlement are constant. Those which I have chosen to illustrate the course of the Paris Conference of 1919 are familiar: geography, justice, politics. Every historical peace negotiation is inevitably based upon geography, since land and material wealth has been a fundamental objective of warring nations. The stakes of diplomacy are the same over the ages. The professed zeal of the negotiators in search of justice in the settlement is far from new. It was proclaimed as loudly when the Congress of Vienna convened a century previous as it was in Wilsonian war aims. Equally, every

From Charles Seymour, *Geography, Justice, and Politics at the Paris Conference of 1919* (New York, 1951), pp. 4–24. Reprinted by permission of the American Geographical Society.

process of peace-making is vitally affected by the factor of politics, the pursuit of self-interest, and since the groups involved are nations, a national self-interest.

But although these factors are not new, they assumed fresh significance in the Paris Conference. The quality and range of the geographical material at its disposal and the stress laid upon it in discussion exceeded anything in preceding diplomatic gatherings. In this situation the influence of Isaiah Bowman as geographer became of international importance. The Conference was significant also because the appeal to justice was not merely fervid but manifestly sincere and constantly reiterated, a new event in modern history. In the third place, the character, complexity, and number of the political interests involved in the drafting of a world settlement at the end of the first World War, distinguish the Conference from any of its predecessors.

Between the principle of justice, using the term in a general sense, and that of political interest there is bound to be conflict. The latter implies a selfishness, a sacred egoism, as the Italians expressed it; which in international affairs cannot always afford to respect the rights of others. The history of the Peace Conference illustrates such an inevitable conflict. But we should not overdramatize or oversimplify it. Certain historians have taken for the *leitmotif* of the negotiations a struggle between simple-minded justice on the one hand and avid greed on the other, between right and wrong, between a virtuous straightforward program designed for the welfare of free peoples and an evil tortuous diplomacy perpetuating a Machiavellian tradition.

The simplicity of this picture of a duel, essentially between the American principle of an equitable free democracy and the European of an outworn intriguing diplomacy, while it appeals to the imagination, does not accord with the facts. There were manifest a good many indications of self-interest in American proposals and no little idealism in various aspects of the European. One historian, commenting on Winston

Churchill, who was the last to forget British interests, reminds us: "that on the very night of the armistice his thoughts veered sympathetically to the stricken foe. Let it be remembered that Winston Churchill at that moment desired to send six fat food-ships to Hamburg." There was never an issue at the Conference in which the terms of the conflict could be expressed in black and white, as right versus wrong.

Nevertheless there was a basic conflict reflecting an essential difference of purpose between the Americans and Europeans and one that goes back to the earlier difference in our attitude toward the war itself. It stemmed as much from a different geographical position as from political philosophy. Both sides desired to establish security, and they were able sincerely to agree upon Wilson's expression of essential purpose: "What we seek," said Wilson, "is the reign of law based upon the consent of the governed and sustained by the organized opinion of mankind." But in their search for this sort of security there was an opposition of emphasis between the New World and the Old. Wilson believed that permanent security could be attained only through a strictly even-handed treatment of each people, strong or weak, friends or enemies. "The impartial justice meted out," he insisted, "must involve no discrimination between those to whom we wish to be just and those to whom we do not wish to be just. It must be a justice that plays no favorites and knows no standards but the equal rights of the several peoples concerned. No special or separate interest of any single nation or any group of nations can be made the basis of any part of the settlement which is not consistent with the common interest of all."

The European states, large and small, and especially the smaller states, were disinclined to take issue with the spirit of this principle; but obviously, when it came to its practical application, factors were raised which contained every element of discord in the interpretation of justice. The surest road to security, the Europeans felt, lay primarily on a reasonable adjustment of conflicting political interests. About those interests the Americans knew very little at first hand, and Europe was not inclined, after the initial expression of emotion had evaporated, to accept blindly Wilson's decision as to what was just and what was unjust.

The Italians could not admit the justice of an Adriatic settlement that left them exposed to the power of the Yugoslavs, an expanding state on the eastern shore. The French, after successive secular assaults from the German enemy across the Rhine, felt that it was only just that they should protect themselves for the future. "The Continental Powers," wrote a liberal British diplomatist, "desired a solution which would satisfy not their greed (there was, whatever may be said to the contrary, comparatively little avidity in Paris) but their anxiety." Every government felt that justice to its own people demanded a protection of national security; and this protection frequently could be achieved only at the expense of another people. Nor could the British Dominions, supported by the mother country as well as the Japanese, understand the justice of turning back her colonies to a Germany which had proved herself both aggressive and unwilling to respect the rights of native populations.

There was in all this a discord of claims which had to be settled by political adjustment or, if you will, by a policy of give and take, the very method of mutual compensations, of back-scratching, which Wilson had banished from his program. This was, he believed, simply the perpetuation of the vicious system which would lead straight to another war; he was convinced, as Lippmann points out, that the war just ended arose out of causes "that were hatched in a sinister system and a tortuous diplomacy."

Each side, whether stressing justice or political interest, appealed to the geographer for assistance. Geography, while it was not qualified to serve as a referee, did become an essential handmaid. For Wilson it was vital to know who the populations were

whose freedom would be determined by new boundaries and how those boundaries would affect their emotional and their economic welfare. As he insisted, the wishes and needs of these peoples transcended everything else. For the other side it was of equal importance that these same facts should be at hand, in order clearly to determine the effect of new frontiers upon the balance of political interest.

Thus geography came into its own, and in the process of educating the statesmen it was fortunate that the necessary materials were at hand. We take a justified pride in the fact that Dr. Bowman played a role of the first importance in this education of the leaders. Mr. Wilson himself profited. It was only on the *George Washington* that, to his surprise, he learned that there was a great mass of Germans in northern Bohemia. "Why," he said, "Masaryk never told me that." Lloyd George discovered, with the help of geographers, the location of Teschen and the difference between Cilicia and Silesia. Toward the end of the Conference the statesmen's interest in and knowledge of maps was sufficient to guarantee a passing grade on a reasonably stiff examination.

One of the most picturesque scenes of the Conference took place in Mr. Wilson's drawing-room in Paris, with the President on all fours in front of a large map on the parquet floor, other plenipotentiaries in like posture, with Orlando crawling like a bear to get a better view, as Wilson delivered a succinct and accurate lecture on the economics and physiography of the Klagenfurt Basin. Maps were everywhere. They were not all good. Westermann refers to certain maps introduced by claimants in the Near East which it would be "a bitter derision to publish." But the appeal to the map in every discussion was constant. When the Supreme Council set up the provisions of the plebiscite in Silesia it gave the order that there should be taken into account the "geographical and economic conditions of the locality."

As for Clemenceau, uninterested as he was in geographical detail, there was no one who perceived more clearly the relations of geography and political power in their larger strategic aspects. The essence of his policy concerned the defence of France. For her protection from the assault of a revivified Germany he recognized two key positions: first, a demilitarized Rhineland on the German western frontier; second, a fortified bastion in Bohemia under Czechoslovakia as an ally of France. "He who holds Bohemia controls Central Europe."

I remember vividly a talk with Clemenceau in the summer of 1925, as he discussed the Locarno Pacts. He had pulled out a map of Central Europe and put his forefinger on Bohemia and his thumb on the Rhineland. "Look," he said, "so long as Germany is contained on the Rhine she cannot expose her western front by a move against the stronghold of the Czechs. These are the critical points, the Rhineland and Bohemia. That is security. But if Germany is allowed to fortify the Rhineland, then she will move against Bohemia, will be free to raise the issue of the Sudetenland, settle the question of Anschluss, and take off in any direction she may decide. For the moment," he added, "we are secure, but I fear that weaker men are going to follow me." He put the safety of France on a geographic foundation.

The difference or conflict, if you will, between the European and the American attitude had to be resolved, if treaties of peace were to be made. It was clear that Wilson could not impose his point of view without certain concessions. It was unfortunate, perhaps inevitable, that the atmosphere in which negotiations took place was not conducive to unemotional reason and blurred the nature of those concessions.

The Paris Conference was called upon not merely to make treaties with defeated enemies but was also supposed to lay down the basis of a durable peace. It was assumed to have full powers. Actually it was subject to forces beyond its control. It met in the atmosphere of bitter belligerency. Despite the signing of an armistice, all the emotions of war persisted; passionate hatred and un-

reasoning anxiety underlay all the decisions taken. Suggestions of fair play to the enemy, who was always the enemy, were met with the short but effective retort of "pro-Boche." Hence much of the vindictive spirit of the final treaties. For treaties do not create conditions; they reflect them.

The difficulties of the peacemakers were intensified by the responsibilities thrown upon them of bringing some sort of order out of the chaos that attends the end of a long drawn-out war. They were expected to produce a plan of permanent peace satisfactory to thirty-odd allied states, five enemy states, to say nothing of the neutrals, at the same time that they acted as an executive commission settling the turbulent current affairs of the entire world. At the moment the great war closed a dozen minor wars broke out — Poles and Czechs, Rumanians and Serbs, Austrians and Slovenes, Hungarians and Slovaks. These had to be liquidated, factories and railroads to be reestablished, food and fuel distributed. War was over but peace was not yet at hand. The same men sat in the morning as the Supreme War Council and in the afternoon as the Supreme Council of the Peace Conference.

Most Americans presumably regarded these men, who were determining the fate of the world, as all-powerful. They represented the victors. The illusion was fostered as you watched them in council and reflected upon the completeness of the triumph to which they had led their peoples. Clemenceau, even in the darkest days of 1917 always the dauntless apostle of victory, presiding in his squat black cutaway and square boots and eternally grey-gloved hands, dry and cruel in his rapier-like wit, so sharp that it took the recipient seconds to realize that he was wounded; Wilson, poised and reassured by the homage of the weaker nationalities, with the proper air of a popular professor; Lloyd George and Balfour, at opposite poles of manner, the first on the edge of his chair, enthusiastic and mercurial, incredibly ignorant of continental history, but intuitively shrewd in his judgment of political issues; Balfour, with his head on the back of his chair and several yards of leg stretched out in front, apparently indifferent, but with a background of historical and philosophical wisdom that made him intellectually the most distinguished man of the Conference; the Italians — Orlando, jovial, generous and ineffective; Sonnino, with his hooked nose and jutting jaw, avid in his nationalism; the two Japanese, their eyes fixed on their maps, responding to all questions with a monosyllabic "Yes." Here the political power of the world was gathered.

But actually these men were by no means all-powerful. There is a price to be paid for democratic diplomacy. Had they been as wise as Nestor they were still responsible to the people back home. It was the paradox of this war waged in the cause of democracy that the very triumph of democracy gave to chauvinistic public opinion a power to determine policies which were destined to sow the seeds of another war, waged again to save democracy.

Hence the difficulties of Lloyd George and Clemenceau endeavoring, as Harold Nicolson put it, "to find the middle way between the desires of their own democracies and the more moderate dictates of their own experience, as well as a middle way between the theology of President Wilson and the practical needs of a distracted Europe." When Lloyd George preached a moderation of the German terms, the Northcliffe Press howled at his heels. Clemenceau, in order to save his government from overthrow was forced to insert the guilt clause in the German treaty and by his compromise in the Rhineland lost his chance of becoming President of the French Republic. Orlando, when he came back to Rome without Fiume, was ousted from the Italian premiership. The disavowal of Wilson by the American Senate was ratified by the American people in the election of 1920.

The Peace Conference, representing the democracies, reflected the mind of the age; it could not rise measurably above its source.

That mind was dominated by a reactionary nostalgia and a traditional nationalism. After four years of turmoil, there was a longing for something solid; after the price each nation had paid in the war, there was a demand for tangible compensation in the peace. Nor can we Americans claim as a nation to have been more far-seeing and altruistic. The Senate debates were tinged with pure national self-interest. It was all thought of in terms of nineteenth century security and prosperity. It is interesting and depressing to consider that probably the most representative man of his age was President Harding calling for a return to "normalcy."

Could the Conference have produced the leadership that would compel the world to a progressive outlook? The case of Woodrow Wilson is instructive. The prophet of an idealistic crusade, he was emphatic in his determination that the peace treaties should point the way to a new path and prepare the world for a new organization. In a small conference of advisers on the *George Washington* on his way to the Conference, he insisted that if it failed he would be ashamed to return to America, "would look around for an out-of-the-way spot, Guam perhaps, to retire to. . . . The world," he said, "is faced by a task of terrible proportions and only the adoption of a cleansing process can recreate or regenerate the world." There was in his voice an impressive sincerity and determination. Here was a man who was marching breast forward.

Wilson's confidence depended upon his faith in the common man. He distrusted the European governments. He believed that his own program voiced a popular feeling that was not merely right, but would prove irresistible. "The American delegates," he said, and it probably could not be said of all the folks at home in America, "will be the only disinterested people at the Peace Conference and the men with whom we are about to deal do not represent their own people. . . . Unless the Conference is prepared to follow the opinions of mankind and to express the will of the people rather than that of their leaders at the Conference, we shall soon be involved in another break-up of the world, and when such a break-up comes it will not be a war but a cataclysm."

Consider how right the presidential prophet was in his long-term view and how wrong in his judgment of the immediate situation. Despite the enthusiasm of the initial greetings given him by the peoples of Europe, his confidence in them was ill-justified. When, in the controversy over Fiume, Wilson followed the method he had tried on various occasions in his university and political career, that of direct appeal to the voice of the people, he was roughly disabused. The burst of popular indignation that followed his Fiume manifesto made clear that the people of Italy were more selfishly nationalistic than their own leaders. When he made a similar appeal to the American people after his return from Paris, the response was no more farsighted or generous.

Wilson, in his fight for justice as against national self-interest, was thus cruelly handicapped, as he himself realized only when the struggle was over. He had a choice between concession to European opinion and the alternative of withdrawing the American delegation from the Conference. The threat of the latter was a powerful weapon in his hands, all the more so because of Europe's need of the financial and economic aid of America. But if it failed and if Wilson left the Conference to stew in its own juice, his dream of world confederation founded upon justice would be shattered. Bit by bit he was brought to a policy of concession, more and more placing faith in a League of Nations as an instrument to correct what seemed to him relatively minor injustice.

Thus the struggle came to be waged on a ground with which he was not familiar and with certain disadvantages increasingly apparent. The program of his Fourteen Points was not well suited to serve as the basis of a practicable settlement nor of a permanent American foreign policy. They had been designed, you will remember,

with an eye to propaganda, especially to persuading the Bolsheviks to keep Russia in the war against Germany. Precise as some of the points were, taken as a whole and with his later declarations, they were subject to conflicting interpretation. The Germans, the allies, Wilson's own delegation, could not be sure what they meant in their specific application. No one at Paris, or at home for that matter, was clear as to the meaning of the commitments that had been made. More than that, no one was sure whether the Fourteen Points applied only to Germany or whether a *sotte voce* reservation regarding Austrian territory which had been made by Italy previous to the armistice, was in fact valid.

Uncertainty of purpose was further confused by looseness of phraseology. At the Congress of Vienna Talleyrand is said to have remarked: "The best principle is to have none." The Paris Conference freely bandied about all sorts of principles, but without defining them or recognizing that they might be mutually at variance: "Democracy," "Viability," "Self-Determination." Democracy was our goal, but it was very vaguely considered in nineteenth century terms without any attempt to reinterpret it in terms of the industrial conditions of southeastern Europe or of the twentieth century conditions of the western peoples.

Did the principle of justice permit the separation of East Prussia from Germany by the Polish corridor, or did it demand that Poland be excluded from access to the sea and Polish populations be left under German rule? The principle of viability pointed toward the decision that Czechoslovakia be allowed to maintain the historic Bohemian frontier; the principle of self-determination demanded with equal force that the frontier be altered, so as to throw the German-speaking Bohemian group into the Reich. The failure to define abstract principles in terms applicable to existing conditions gave rise to the suspicion of a lack of principle which weakened Wilson and from which the peacemakers and the treaties never recovered.

When the President met his territorial advisers on the *George Washington*, he gave them an inspiring directive: "Tell me what's right and I'll fight for it. Give me a guaranteed position." But he couldn't tell them how to interpret justice in the case of conflicting rights. The Saar Basin is a purely German territory to which the claim on historic grounds by France is obviously fragile. But its coal offered a ready means of reparation for the wanton damage done by German armies to the French mines at Lens and Valenciennes. Was it right to refuse this reparation to France? Should Danzig, an ancient and a purely German port, be turned over to the new Poland as an essential opening on the sea? Should an economic unit such as the Klagenfurt Basin be ruinously cut in two so that the frontier might conform with ethnographic lines? What to do with a region such as the Banat of Temesvár claimed by both Serbs and Rumanians, but where the nationalities live so intermingled that no recognizable line of demarcation exists? In each such case any decision was bound to evoke from the disappointed party the complaint of injustice. There was always the danger that in correcting an old injustice a new grievance would be created.

Wilson's negotiating position was weakened not merely by such uncertainties but by certain unforeseen developments. He himself made a vital mistake at the very start, by conceding to Orlando in a private conversation the frontier of the Brenner. There could be no more obvious infraction of his own Point Nine which provided for "clearly recognizable lines of nationality." Immediately the word was whispered about that the President didn't quite mean what he said. It was not unnatural later that the Italians should put in their claim to Fiume; and when the President, having also yielded to British and French demands, refused further concessions in the Adriatic, Sonnino could complain that Wilson, having lost his virginity to Clemenceau and Lloyd George, was now attempting to regain virtue at the expense of Italy. Once Wilson began to yield it was difficult to find a place to stop.

Vital to an understanding of these concessions to European political self-interest are the negotiations of the League of Nations Covenant. At his first conference with Lloyd George and Clemenceau in London, the President, with an honest naïveté, as Clemenceau would call it in his famous speech, a *noble candeur*, made plain his faith in the League of Nations as the keystone of the entire settlement. He thereby placed in the hands of the Europeans a very strong card. They would support the League as Wilson's instrument of justice, but they would expect his understanding and support in the particular problems of political interest which they themselves faced. As Wilson more and more turned to the League as a corrective of inevitable injustice they could use it more and more as an instrument of pressure.

The United States Senate played into their hands. When Wilson, following his visit home in February, returned to Paris he brought with him American amendments to the Covenant. Could he expect the Europeans to accept these without a *quid pro quo*? When, with the Monroe Doctrine amendment to the Covenant in his hands, the Japanese produced theirs on racial equality, which in the climate of American opinion he could not possibly accept, his negotiating position on Shantung was undermined.

News from the United States did not help. When Wilson spoke to the Europeans about the moral force of public opinion they were in a position to ask how far he represented the voice of America. They, at least, had received solid majorities in their recent elections, while the American voters of November previous had sent a hostile majority to Congress. More and more Europe asked itself whether the republic of the New World really was ready to commit itself to a fulfillment of the Wilsonian program of justice. It was safer, perhaps, for the Old World to rely upon a reasonable adjustment of political interests. It is possible to portray the outcome of

Wilson's struggle for justice as a bankruptcy of effort. It has been suggested that his own nervous breakdown in the autumn of 1919 was the result of his fruitless hope of convincing himself and the world that the settlement was based upon principles of justice, when in his heart he knew that this was not true. Certainly the gulf between what was apparently promised in the Fourteen Points and what actually transpired was both broad and deep.

This failure, as I have suggested, was not entirely caused by politics, by the selfish interests of the European powers. The geographers themselves in their own impartial analysis proved the impracticability of fulfilling the justice of Wilson's political and social idealism. "In this modern closely organized, strongly commercialized world," wrote Dr. Bowman, "it is virtually impossible to make a clear-cut distinction between what is right from the standpoint of ethnography, nationalistic sentiment, and abstract justice, and what is fair from the standpoint of economic advantage."

This is not to say that certain of the larger issues were not settled on the basis of purely political interests without regard to either justice or geography. We cannot overlook the violence done to both in the Shantung clauses and in the attempted partition of the Near East. Nor can we forget the even more devastating effects of the short-sightedness that characterized the handling of reparations.

But these unfortunate aspects of the settlement should not blur the sincerity of the attempt to achieve non-political justice. Wilson, on the advice of his territorial advisers led by Bowman, was willing to risk Italian withdrawal from the League by standing firm on Fiume; and where the geographers were given a relatively free hand, as in the European territorial commissions, the Wilsonian program accomplished a higher degree of success than has generally been realized. The frontiers of the new map of Europe conformed more closely with ethnographic divisions than any in previous history. "No one," said

Lord Balfour, who was not given to extravagance, "has ever made a practical suggestion as to how they could be bettered."

The territorial provisions of the treaties were subjected to furious criticism, naturally enough, since none of the claimants could be satisfied; and often by those so ignorant of geography that they scarcely bothered to read the text of the settlement. "The treaty," said Lloyd George, "is the most abused and least perused document of history." But we may note that the European territorial provisions stood up twenty years. When they cracked finally it was not from inherent weakness or injustice but from external assault.

In protection of the territorial settlement the Conference provided two bulwarks of security, very different in nature but capable, for a period at least, of working together to protect the peace. The one was the Wilsonian League of Nations, enfeebled by American abstention and by the exclusion of Germany and Russia; offering promise nonetheless, if it were actively developed, to mobilize Wilson's hopes of the "organized opinion of mankind" into the collective security which he had preached. The other was Clemenceau's strategic security, resting upon a demilitarized Rhineland and Czechoslovak control of Bohemia.

The successors of the peacemakers permitted both of these bulwarks to disintegrate. The failure of the League as an organ of collective security, of reconciliation on the one hand, of resistance to aggression whether in Manchuria or Ethiopia on the other, had by the middle thirties already become manifest to the world. Strategic security disappeared in 1936, when Hitler marched into the Rhineland unopposed and began the construction of the Siegfried Line. Henceforth, with his western flank secure, he was free to move against Bohemia, incorporate Austria, and launch his next aggression as he saw fit.

So shattering have been the events of the past two decades that today we seem to face an entirely different set of circumstances than those that attended the close of the first World War. Without question external conditions have been altered in a revolutionary sense. The development of communications, of the airplane and radio, has annihilated distance. Science has shown us new ways to produce wealth, to preserve life, and to destroy life. New forms of social philosophy and action have been developed, powerful to alleviate the suffering of the less fortunate, but capable also of creating a tyranny that might obliterate the individual freedom which is the hope of mankind. The lines that define friends and foes have shifted; our allies of yesterday are the enemies of today.

To these changes we must adjust ourselves. But human impulses have not changed. The basic factors that underlie international relations are constant. The assurance of security, the acquisition of power, are always shaping the course of foreign policy, whether you are looking for the control of gold, or wheat, or oil, or uranium. So long as the existing international system persists, a country will always demand the critical materials.

Because the basic factors are unchanged the conduct of foreign affairs must be more than courageous; it must also be a steady continuity. A peace conference is not an isolated event where permanent magic can be achieved. There is no treaty that can of itself serve as an adequate basis for peace, unless its principles are carried forward actively year by year. You cannot rest on your oars and pray for normalcy. It was not so much the absence of justice from the Paris Peace Conference that caused the ultimate debacle; it was the failure to make the most of what justice there was. The appalling threat of Russian diplomatic success in the East and in Central Europe has resulted chiefly, as Gordon Wasson points out, from the fact that Russia, over the past three decades, has "hewed close to the line of a hard, cold, consistent policy. This cannot be said of us or of Britain, or of France."

Furthermore the same principles that underlie the conduct of a modern peace conference are valid in the day by day conduct of international affairs. If those principles, properly supported by material and moral power are translated into a steady foreign policy, there is good hope, I believe, that this cold war of the moment may ultimately be liquidated without recourse to World War III. Such a policy, if even a titular peace is to be maintained, implies strength without bluster, negotiation without appeasement. It points ultimately towards an adjustment of conflicting political interests.

That adjustment must be founded upon an intelligent understanding of human geography, of the character of the conflicting peoples, the surroundings in which they live, the material resources of which they dispose, the natural barriers and communications which divide and unite them. Knowledge of geographical facts and understanding of how to use them are essential.

So long as there are nations, selfish national interests are bound to exist. We must take account of them. We must learn to define exactly our own political interest; we must understand clearly and objectively the interests of our allies and of our enemies. No ultimate and permanent adjustment can be made that disregards political interest.

But in that adjustment the principle of justice must play a major and, in the end we may hope, a determining role. Better the physical destruction of humanity by the atom bomb than the elimination of morals from the life of man. The idealistic vision of Woodrow Wilson must always be before our eyes, not merely a vision of justice in the abstract, but one that shall be administered with even hand through the organized co-operation of all the nations of the world. Only thus can there be a permanent assurance of bridging the gap between national self-interest and human justice.

SUGGESTIONS FOR ADDITIONAL READING

The student of the Versailles peace settlement of 1919–1920 will find an abounding literature on the subject. In fact, he will find that more has been written about Versailles than about other historic efforts at international peacemaking.

Moreover, as a result of deliberate governmental directives since about 1920 to publish extensive collections of diplomatic papers, students of twentieth century affairs enjoy the important advantage of having at their disposal the raw materials of the diplomat, the historian, and the foreign relations analyst. Thus, the American diplomatic series, *Papers Relating to the Foreign Relations of the United States. The Paris Peace Conference 1919* (Washington, 1942–47), 13 vols., provides an official record from which it is possible to gain valuable first-hand insights. Similarly the *Documents on British Foreign Policy, 1919–1939,* First Series, E. L. Woodward and R. Butler, eds. (London, 1947–52), 4 vols., furnish the official record of British diplomacy. Among unofficial collections, N. Almond and R. H. Lutz, *The Treaty of St. Germain. A Documentary History of Its Territorial and Political Clauses* (Stanford, 1935), provides great detail on the making of the Austrian treaty, while David Hunter Miller, *My Diary at the Conference of Paris* (New York, 1928), 21 vols., remains a classic source with numerous documents and special emphasis on the origins of the League of Nations Covenant.

In the field of general literature, H. M. V. Temperley, ed., *A History of the Peace Conference of Paris* (London, 1920–24), 6 vols., is a most comprehensive study, covering general conference issues, special territorial and technical problems, as well as all the peace settlements relating to the smaller nations of Europe. F. S. Marston, *The Peace Conference of 1919* (London, 1944), is invaluable as a handbook on the organization, mechanics, and procedures of the peace conference. M. I. Newbigin, *Aftermath, a Geographical Study of the Peace Terms* (London, 1920) gives a convenient summary of territorial changes in 1919, whereas I. Bowman, *The New World* (Yonkers, 1928), 4th ed., is a classic full-length geographic study of the post-1919 world.

A. Luckau, *The German Delegation at the Paris Peace Conference* (New York, 1941), gives a full account of German diplomatic actions in 1919, while by contrast, strong anti-German views are found in a work by the famous student of geopolitics, Sir Halford Mackinder, *Democratic Ideals and Reality* (London, 1919), which appeared at the opening of the peace conference, but attracted surprisingly little international attention.

Descriptions of the political atmosphere prevailing in Paris and of the negotiations which led to inter-allied decisions on final peace terms for victors and vanquished alike can be found in: H. Wickham Steed, *Through Thirty Years* (Garden City, 1925), II; G. B. Noble, *Policies and Opinions at Paris, 1919* (New York, 1935); E. M. House and C. Seymour, *What Really Happened At Paris* (New York, 1921), which includes accounts by various members of the American delegation; C. H. Haskins and R. H. Lord, *Some Problems of the Peace Conference* (Cambridge, Mass., 1920); James T. Shotwell, *At the Paris Peace Conference* (New York, 1937), a fairly critical account by a leading American delegation expert; G. A. Riddell, *Lord Riddell's Intimate Diary of the Peace Conference and After, 1918–1923* (London, 1923).

How did some of the leading makers of the Versailles settlement evaluate their handiwork? French interpretations may be gleaned from the accounts of Premier Georges Clemenceau, *Grandeur and Misery of Victory* (New York, 1930); British views from Prime Minister David Lloyd George, *The Truth About the Peace Treaties* (London, 1938), 2 vols., and Churchill; American views from Secretary of State Robert Lansing, *The Big Four* (Cambridge, Mass., 1921) and Charles Seymour, *The Intimate Papers of Colonel House* (Boston, 1926–28), 4 vols.; Italian views from Premier Francesco Nitti, *The Decadence of Europe* (London, 1923).

For detailed discussion and interpretations of reparations and the economic bases of the peace see: P. M. Burnett, *Reparation at the Paris Peace Conference from the Standpoint of the American Delegation* (New York, 1940), 2 vols. an objective scholarly treatment; Bernard Baruch, then American delegate on economic matters, *The Making of the Reparation and Economic Sections of the Treaty* (New York, 1920); Karl Bergmann, *The History of Reparations* (Boston, 1927), a balanced German study of the subject.

For special political and territorial problems which merit particular attention, René Albrecht-Carrié, *Italy at the Paris Peace Conference* (New York, 1938), gives excellent and balanced coverage of the complex issues that beset that major power. See also: T. Komarnicki, *Rebirth of the Polish Republic* (London, 1957); Ian Morrow, *The Peace Settlement in the German-Polish Borderlands* (London, 1936); A. E. Moodie, *The Italo-Yugoslav Boundary* (London, 1945); S. Wambaugh, *Plebiscites Since the World War* (Washington, 1933), 2 vols.; Robert W. Seton-Watson, *Treaty Revision and the Hungarian Frontiers* (London, 1934); W. E. Stephens, *Revisions of the Treaty of Versailles* (New York, 1939) which deals principally with the League, technical organizations, and reparations. S. Bonsal, *Suitors and Suppliants: The Little Nations at Versailles* (New York, 1946), adds journalistic flavor to the vicissitudes of great- and small-power relationships in 1919.

The enduring controversy surrounding the figure of Woodrow Wilson has been given extensive and sympathetic treatment by Ray Stannard Baker in *Woodrow Wilson and World Settlement* (Garden City, New York, 1922), 3 vols., and critical treatment by Thomas A. Bailey in *Woodrow Wilson and The Lost Peace* (New York, 1944).

Finally, the Peace of Versailles warrants evaluation through the historical perspective of the entire interwar period. To this end G. M. Gathorne-Hardy, *A Short History of International Affairs 1920–1939* (London, 1950), 4th ed., provides one of the best concise handbooks, while E. H. Carr's *The Twenty Years' Crisis, 1919–1939* (London, 1939), presents a more interpretive and critical account of the legacy of Versailles. Both works may be profitably complemented with F. P. Walters' detailed study, *A History of the League of Nations* (London, 1952), 2 vols.